Girl Power

Girl Power

Compiled by Phyllis Hodges CFT., LHM

Foreword by Phyllis Yvonne Stickney

Copyright

2020 @ Phyllis Hodges CFT., LHM. All rights reserved. This book or any portion thereof may not be reproduced or used in any manner whatsoever without the express written permission of the publisher or Phyllis Hodges except for the use of brief quotations in a book review.

Printed in the United States of America

First printing, 2020

Hardback ISBN 978-1-951883-15-7

Library of Congress Number 2020916426

Cover Design, Laurence Walden
Illustrator, Kim Yarbrough

Researchers and Organizers
Rose Wright   Ca'Ron Watkins
Candince Hodges   Personal Interviews

Photographers
Ca'Ron Watkins   Caela Fugate
Plan C Video Production   *C.D. Rist*

Global Empowerment, A Woman's Guide to Liberation. Copyright 2019. Anjerrio Kameron. All Rights Reserved.

Girl Power, Living Your Dream. Copyright 2020. Laurence Walden. All Rights Reserved.

This project was funded in part by a grant from the Black History Commission of Arkansas.

Butterfly Typeface Publishing
Little Rock Arkansas

Dedication

This book is dedicated to my mom – Rose Wright, my daughter – Candince Hodges, and my two granddaughters – CaRon Watkins and Jade Crosby. I would be remiss if I did not send a shout-out to all the beautiful and wonderfully made aspiring women in this world.

This book is written for us all.

While reading someone's else story, it may cause you to say, "My life is not so bad after all!" The stories in this book may inspire you to desire love, peace, and happiness.

There are some practical goals you can set towards achieving your dreams, including:

Believe it!

Work at it!

Achieve it!

Remember, it is not about being like someone else; it is about being like yourself!

"Just Be You"

Author Phyllis Hodges CFT., LHM

Table of Contents

Girl Power Is Key 25

    Phyllis Hodges CFT., LHM 25

Not A Time For Silence 31

    Phyllis Hodges 31

A Whole New World 47

    Claudia Elisa Balderas Fountain 47

My Life: How It All Started 63

    Paula Rena Hegler McDore 63

My Story. My Stingers. My Success. 71

    Stacy Moultrie 71

Life After Seventy 87

    Dr. Georgianne Thomas 87

An Answer to a Prayer 97

    Helaine Raye Palmer Williams 97

Multiple Gracious Opportunities 113

    Dr. Marion Williams 113

A Borrowed Girl with No Identity, an "In-between" 123

   Kim Yarbrough 123

Final Thoughts 133

   Girl Power, That's You! 133

About the Author 135

More Girl Power 137

   Arkansas Female Celebrities & Noteworthy Personalities 138

   Cover Ladies 139

   History Makers & Trailblazers 142

   House of Representatives – Arkansas Origin (Male & Female) 143

   Music Makes the World Go Round 144

   The Hall of Faith: Heroes and *Sheroes 146

   Global Empowerment, A Woman's Guide to Liberation 147

   Girl Power: Living Your Dreams 153

   Girl Power Affirmations 155

Foreword

When my fellow Arkansas Author, Phyllis Hodges, asked me to contribute the foreword to this book, I thought, "What can I say to these young females who one day will inherit the responsibilities that we women shoulder today?" I asked myself, "What could someone have told me at such an impressionable age, that would have gotten my attention, something I would receive and **APPLY** to my life continually?"

I imagined myself as your big sister, mother, or aunt, getting you ready to meet your future and preparing you for your destiny, helping you pack your carry-on. What would I tell you to make sure to include in your travel bag?

LOVE was my first thought because love was provided in large quantities in my daily diet at home. The love received there set the tone for how I looked at and approached the world and my place in it.

Learn to love yourself. Pamper yourself with long hot baths, turn off the cell phone at a reasonable hour daily, take slow walks in the park, listen to soft music, and indulge in solo dances with your shadow.

And whatever vessel or package you came to the planet in, learn to love it and embrace it fully.

Always maintain an *Attitude of Gratitude,* no matter what. This will ensure that you can and will make it through anything that life throws your way.

SMILE, LAUGH and **GIGGLE** often - especially at yourself.

READ A GOOD BOOK once a month.

Remember, **GOD IS REAL.** There is a Higher Power, Intelligence, or Spirit that most of us call God, The Creator, or The Most High.

Be aware of the presence and power of **God EVERYWHERE.** Connect through thanksgiving, praise, and prayer, **IMAGINATON**, and **CURIOSITY**.

GIRL POWER is something with which we were born.

It's in our DNA.

USE IT WISELY; there is an expiration date.

Your Aunt in spirit and agape love,

Phyllis Y. Stickney

Acclaim

One of the most important realities in the world is knowing your worth! There are times, because of our strong feminine attributes, we miss the opportunity to celebrate God's undeniable greatness deposited into each one of us!

The power we witness in "Women Who Rock!" didn't miraculously appear overnight; God ordained it while we were yet in our mothers' wombs. Little girls are nurtured to become great women who exemplify femininity at its best, but not without the confrontation of extraneous variables.

Girl Power is indicative of survival and resilience in a world that once denied the very thought of our worth and contributions being important enough to count; therefore, in 1919, because of the Women's Suffrage Movement, we were granted the right to be counted via the 19th Amendment.

We are our sisters' keepers; therefore, God has given us the power to undergird each other in ways unique to human understanding. When women come together and agree, the sky is literally the limit. As we embrace the power God deposits in our lives, a metamorphosis occurs, causing us to transform into more than conquerors!

Remember, it was a woman God ordained to save the baby, Moses. It was a woman who saved the lives of spies sent to Jericho. It was a woman whose efforts saved a race of people in Shushan. It was a woman, serving as the Israelite Judge, who delivered Sisera into Barak's hand. And it was God's divine power working through the Virgin Mary, who brought forth the Savior of the world. I would be remiss if I did not celebrate the courageous women who rose early one morning to attend to Jesus but found an empty tomb, and because of their love, faith, and commitment, were rewarded with the charge of exclaiming the Good News of Christ's Resurrection!

We praise and honor God for blessing us with "Girl Power!"

Shirley J. Inkton

Itinerant Elder, African Methodist Episcopal Church, 12th District

Author, Strength for Life's Journey

Arkansas State Chaplain, Delta Sigma Theta Sorority, Inc.

Acknowledgments

Several wonderful people contributed in countless ways to the creation of this book. These "World Changers" are here to encourage, enlighten, motivate and empower all females. These ladies set the bar high:

Claudia Fountain

Paula Mcdore

Stacy Moultrie

Dr. Georgianne Thomas

Helaine Williams

Dr. Marion Williams

Kim Yarbrough

Now let us follow their lead!

Thanks to my friend, the one and only, most creative, talented artist, and musician that I know, Laurence Walden (AKA – Blinky). This book cover (front and back) is everything that I desired.

To my new friend, Kim Yarbrough: I remember the day I first met you and listened as you spoke about your desires, needs, passions, and talents. I knew right away that this was a partnership of **true** *Girl Power*. When I saw your many illustrations, I imagined working with you and knew that I wanted to showcase your work in my book.

Sincere gratitude goes out to my wonderful family for being so supportive while I spent numerous hours researching and interviewing contributors.

To my team members, LaShawna Poe and Michelle Philmon, your hard work has paid off.

Byron, my soulmate, husband, lover, friend, and confidant, your patience and prayers will never be forgotten.

Mom, your shoulders and listening ears have been just what the "doctor" ordered during this season of my life.

Ca'Ron, my sweet granddaughter, this book would not be complete without all your hard work and sacrifices.

Candince, my one and only first-born daughter, you helped me when I was having writers' cramps and when I was climbing the walls.

Iris M. Williams (Butterfly Typeface Publishing), I can only say, "God Sent You to Me!"

Girl Power: Supporting Friends

Lincoln Heritage Funeral Advantage Whole Life Insurance - Managers, Stephen Benson & Dale Sherman

Evonne's Inspirations, LLC - Evonne Amerine

Nichol's Knights Productions - LouWendy Jenkins CEO & Founder

Carolyn Ann Cato - Colclough

Thelma Shorter

D3 Health & Fitness - Dr. Angela Dallas, Health & Wellness Coach

Shorter College - S.W.E.P

LaShawna Poe

Healing Touch Outreach Prayer Ministry

Roosevelt, Kiffanie, Rashad, Kalia & Kiersten Walker

Ms. Joy M., Reverend & Sisters - "Sisters Love"

Ruby H - U.D.B.A. H/W- Chair

Dr. Pamela J. Randolph - Girls in Pearls CDCE

Kristian Nelson - Hawgz Blues Cafe

Carousel Fit 4 Life Wellness - On The GO

In memory of two special people who lost their lives to Covid-19:

Norris Sam (10-7-1932 to 6-17-2020)
Rodney McNair "Binx" Watts (5-2-1945 to 8-7-2020)

RIP Ecclesiastes 3:1-2

Girl Power Defined

(English Version)

Girl power endures, and it comes to play in the bad times. The power is the strength to get up and raise her hands to her help from the Almighty God.

Girl power declares life, to that, which has none.

Girl power doesn't give up and believes even if it is not seen or heard.

Girl power places goals to finish them and has another one ready to go.

Girl power hears the voice of God speak the word over her life, to change the atmosphere.

Girl power faces fears with the greater one in her.

Girl power is a power to love that is placed because God loved us first and showed nurturing to women as mothers, sisters, and friends.

Girl power is a movement of faith.

Girl power is the breakthrough liberation of all lines of repeated patterns and creates a new life, revived as Jesus Christ.

Girl power is not staying stuck but moving to get things done.

Girl power is changing the perspective, the situation.

Girl power forgives to have peace.

Girl power is discerning with wisdom.

Girl power is won through warfare experience!

Uvalilia Flores
Translator/Servant of God - Tucson, Arizona

Girl Power Defined

(Spanish Version)

El poder de la mujer resiste, es practicado en los malos momentos, el poder es la fuerza de levantarse y estirar las manos a su ayuda del Dios todopoderoso.

El poder de la mujer declara la vida, a eso, que no tiene vida.

El poder de la mujer no se rinde y cree, incluso cuando no se ve ni se escucha.

El poder de la mujer pone metas para terminarlas y tiene otra lista.

El poder de la mujer escucha la voz de Dios, habla la palabra sobre su vida para cambiar la atmósfera.

El poder de la mujer enfrenta temores con el mayor que esta en ella.

El poder de la mujer es el poder de amar porque Dios nos amó primero y nos mostró su crianza ahora nosotras como madres, hermanas y amigas.

El poder de la mujer es un movimiento de fe.

El poder de la mujer es la liberación revolucionaria de todas las líneas de patrones repetidas y crea una nueva vida, revivida como Jesucristo.

El poder de la mujer no se queda estancada, sino que se mueve para hacer las cosas.

El poder de la mujer cambia la perspectiva, la situación.

El poder de la mujer perdona para tener paz.

El poder de la mujer es discernir con sabiduría.

¡El poder de la mujer se gana a través de la experiencia de guerra!

Uvalilia Flores
Translator/Servant of God - Tucson, Arizona

Let's Talk!

This book is born out of my desire to share some phenomenal stories with you. I believe that we all have something to say. We all have a story!

I decided to shine the spotlight on seven beautiful ladies from around the globe who have an Arkansas connection. (I've included my story as well!)

As a matter of fact, before you get into the reading of this book, I would like to speak to you about the woman who wrote my foreword, Phyllis Yvonne Stickney. Phyllis is a multi-talented comedian, actress, and celebrity from Arkansas. You may remember her from her roles in the following movies: *How Stella Got Her Groove Back*, *Brewster's Place* and *What's Love Got to Do with It?*

I had the amazing opportunity to see Phyllis personally at one of Little Rock's Community Centers. She was performing Spoken Word and was phenomenal. It was an extraordinary performance. I had heard about Spoken Word, but this was my first live experience for this type show! Wow, it was almost breathtaking. The voices, the music, and the body language were something to witness. And to know she was from Little Rock, Arkansas, my home state, made me so proud.

Highlighted in this book are not only historical people but also moments and places. When you think of Arkansas, sometimes you cannot imagine the beautiful parks, bike trails, historical spots, and even the successful individuals who were born and raised in the beautiful state of Arkansas. There have also been several movies filmed here!

I love journaling and sharing my history as well as the stories of others. As African Americans, we must be careful when it comes to our history. So much of our history has been lost or forgotten. I think this has happened on purpose in many cases. It is essential to know who we are and from whence we came. Learning about our ancestral background is imperative. With that in mind, after you've finished reading this book, I encourage you to take time and ask your family and friends questions about their history. I think you'll be surprised at what you have been missing!

After reading the stories of these uniquely talented ladies, I assure you, you will be motivated to get up, learn more, and to do more. It is never too late to help yourself, improve your flaws, and reach for higher goals. We all have room for improvement in our lives. It only takes one person to believe in you and catapult you to the next level in your life. Of course, there will be **HATERS**!

I laugh because I think we all need haters to push us into our wealthy place. Remember, no one can stop you from living your best life, but you. So do not get in your way!

Make a mental note of how many of these ladies experienced a setback on the way to their comeback! Success is not easy, but it's worth it!

What makes you happy? Are you doing it?

If not, ask yourself, "Why not?"

Look in the mirror and ask tough questions such as, "Do I love me? Do I *really* love who I see in the mirror?"

I placed a symbolic mirror on the back cover of this book so that when you see these beautiful and famous ladies, you will not wish to look like them or to be them. Instead, I want you to look in the mirror and see and be who God created you to be.

I placed myself on the cover next to these extraordinary ladies because I believe in myself and love who God created me to be. I put my beautiful mom on the cover because while so many people identify with famous people as their hero, my mom is my hero. She was the first and best teacher I ever had!

I **LOVE** this lady.

This book is designed to educate you. It talks about economic development, mental health (including depression), physical health, social justice, and relationships. *Girl Power* is a platform to help you reach your best potential.

There is power in our words. We all need to learn to celebrate each other. The Bible talks about a person lacking friends, and when that is the case, we should show ourselves friendly. Check out who is in your circle. I honestly believe *iron sharpens iron*. Everyone in your circle should bring something to the table, if not, you may need to reevaluate your circle. What do you have in common with your friends or your *bestie* as we say these days? I am a firm believer that you should be your own **BEST FRIEND,** and this is what encourages *Girl Power*.

I believe God encouraged me to share these stories because these women (including myself) have something to say. Like most of us, there is a story *shut up in our bones*, and it needs to be exposed.

My friend Kim, the illustrator, has so many gifts and talents. We decided to intertwine them to help our readers. Kim's drawings will motivate you artists to pick up that sketch pad and get to work.

Some of these history-makers will be trailblazers for some of you.

Yes, you can do this.

Remember, your gift will make room for you?

Move over and start writing or get with one of us to serve as your mentor. We all need a **MENTOR**! Nothing just happens. You must go after it, be persistent.

Do you *really* think you are reading this book by chance?

It is your time to get busy. You can do it!

You are smart, gifted, and talented. You deserve a chance – even if it is nothing more than learning how to take time for yourself. Enjoy this season of your life.

In closing, what have you done recently to help someone? Next, what do you think it would take to make you happy?

Read these stories and realize nothing is easy. It does not happen overnight. But these ladies accomplished some of their dreams, and they are continuing to dream. So, it is your turn.

Go, make yourself happy. Do not depend on anyone to do it for you. If it is to be, it is up to you.

And remember, there are plenty of people who are willing to help you achieve your goal.

Author Phyllis Hodges CFT., LHM

#GIRLPOWER

Girl Power Is Key

Phyllis Hodges CFT., LHM

These great ladies you will soon read about are extraordinary, one of a kind, risk-takers, which many may not know. But after reading their stories, your lives will be changed forever. I have a special connection with each one of them. During our interviews, I was encouraged to dig deep and search for more women of their kind. Everyone has a story to tell, so I encourage you to take this book to heart, learn from your mistakes, and realize we all make them. We all have trials and tribulations. Realize that God is not a respecter of persons. If He made a way of escape for these ladies to climb to the top, to survive, and to witness greatness, He will provide for you as well.

While reading and enjoying *Girl Power*, check out all the beautiful and unique illustrations of the beautiful queens drawn by artist and contributor, Kim Yarbrough.

Girl Power

Vanessa Williams (Born March 18, 1963)

American actress, singer, and fashion designer

The First African American, Miss America 1984

Term: September 17, 1983-July 22, 1984 (resigned)

Titles held: Miss America 1984, Miss New York 1983, & Miss Syracuse 1983

Vanessa Williams initially gained recognition as the first African American winner of the Miss America title when she was crowned Miss America 1984 in September 1983. Vanessa won the Preliminary Swimsuit and the Preliminary Talent portions with a vocal performance of "Happy Days Are Here Again."

Several weeks before the end of her reign, however, a scandal arose when Penthouse magazine bought and published unauthorized nude photographs of Williams. Williams was pressured to relinquish her title and was succeeded by the First Runner-Up, Miss New Jersey 1983 Suzette Charles.

Vanessa was the first Miss America to give up her crown. Thirty-two years later, in September 2015, when Williams served as head judge for the Miss American 2016 pageant, former Miss American CEO Sam Haskell made a public apology to her and her mom for the event of 1984.

Her 10-month reign made more history for her and the pageant system. It was the first resignation in the history of the pageant. Vanessa went on to receive 11 Grammys, star in Ugly Betty, and appear on Broadway.

Girl Power

Introducing Phyllis Hodges ...

Someone once said, "If you want to make the Lord laugh, tell Him your plans."

Adding my story wasn't part of the plan for this book. However, after reconsidering one of the original contributors, it became necessary.

Now that it is done, it makes perfect sense to me to add my story since it was my vision (God-inspired) to compile a book about women who inspire other women.

If you know me, then you know that I enjoy talking to people and encouraging them to live their best life not only physically, but emotionally as well. As a fitness guru, I encounter many people (particularly women) who put themselves last on their task list. Sometimes they do not even put themselves on the list. Ladies, this will never do.

We must take time to nourish our bodies as well as our minds. Eat right, exercise, and fuel your mind with literature and sounds that edify your spirit.

In the times we are living in now, this is so especially important as many of our lives have changed drastically. As we embrace our new normal, take time to reflect on what was and then decide on what will be.

It is my prayer that you will allow *Girl Power* to assist you in your journey!

Please turn the page to learn more about me and my personal story.

Not A Time For Silence

Phyllis Hodges

The decision to share my story was a last-minute one. While providing a platform for other women to share their amazing stories, I realized I had a story to tell as well. The stories of the phenomenal women I chose will encourage and uplift you. I pray that mine will as well. Inspiration is especially needed during these challenging times and especially for females.

I pray for a successful outcome for all who contributed and all who will read.

As the submissions came in, I read each one carefully, making sure their story was in line with the purpose of the book. I was excited to find that they were. However, later I found disappointing and disturbing information on social media from one of the original contributors. Her comments seem to contradict the very principle of *Girl Power*.

Among other things, *Girl Power* stands for unity, love, encouragement, and power.

Unfortunately, her contribution to the book was not chosen. While freedom of speech is afforded to each of us, I believe considering the impact of your words is very important. The lives and feelings of people matter. Ask yourself, "Does what I have to say enhance the world or feed into the negativity that surrounds us?"

We are commanded to interact with others in love and treat them as we would want to be treated. There is no place for bigotry and hate in our world. Violence of any kind (physical, verbal, or written) is unacceptable.

Unfortunately, due to racial profiling, hate crimes, and police brutality, many blacks and people of color are experiencing the effects of deep-seated prejudices.

Now is not the time for silence. Now is the time to open our mouths and give voice to the injustices that we witness. This is the first step in eradicating the harmful behaviors of others.

When someone says, "I don't see color," ask them, "What does that mean?"

When you hear, "Make America great again," ask for an explanation.

If you're told, "You don't sound black," ask for clarification.

Comments like, "All lives matter," and "I can't be racist because my friend is black," and "You're so articulate" can be harmful and need to be addressed. The people who speak these words may need to be educated.

Let's be clear, subtle racism (i.e., white silence, discriminatory lending, mass incarceration, racist mascots, anti-affirmative action, hiring and housing discrimination, limited access to health care, racial profiling, denial of white privilege, prioritizing white voices as experts, anti-immigration policies, and pay inequality, etc.) should not be tolerated. It is time we use our voices and our votes to make a change in our world so that everyone can feel loved and not feel afraid.

Girl Power: Phyllis Hodges

As an African American woman, I feel the *Girl Power* love and strength I carry with me daily.

In 1974, I was sixteen when I met my soulmate and future husband. He was 22 years old and white. This charming, blond hair, bow-legged man drove a red convertible sports car. I was working my first job after school at Kentucky Fried Chicken (KFC), located off Broadway street in Little Rock, Arkansas. I later learned he had moved to Little Rock to attend College at UALR.

I can remember it like it was yesterday. Every evening he would stop by Kentucky Fried Chicken and order a 5-piece Jumbo Box with cream potatoes and gravy, coleslaw, a biscuit, and a drink. One evening as I was taking his order with a pen and pad (remember it was 1974, so there were no computers), fate intervened. My pen stopped working.

"Here," he offered me his pen. "You can use mine."

He was such a gentleman, and I was impressed.

"When you finish taking my order," he continued. "Write down your number, too, please."

His statement both surprised and flattered me.

I wrote down a number for him, but it wasn't my home number. I was only 16, and I still lived with my mom. He drove off, and a time later the phone at the restaurant rang. (Yes, I gave him the number to the restaurant.)

I was called to the phone and was surprised again. It was the handsome gentleman calling. It wasn't that I didn't think he would call; I just didn't expect him to call so soon!

We talked for about a minute, and then he asked if he could come to see me.

"I live with my mom," I said.

"I don't have a problem with that," he responded.

Persistent and determined, he called my mom right away.

This is the part of my story that I want young readers and mothers to pay attention to and understand. Moms, it is so important to get to know who has the attention of your girls. Girls, the guy who is interested in you, should want to know who your parents are and respect you enough to be able to communicate that with you.

"Mrs. Wright," he began. "My name is Byron Hodges. I just met your daughter Phyllis at KFC, and I'd like to come visit her at your home."

Later mom told me that Byron was so polite that she had to meet him to see if what he presented on the telephone was indeed real.

"That's fine," Mom agreed, "But it has to be when I'm here."

"I understand," Byron said, "But there is one problem."

"And what is that?" Mom asked.

"I'm white," Byron told her.

"Well," Mom said with laughter in her voice. "That's your problem, not mine."

Ever since that day, Bryon considered himself Mom's son and part of our family. Was it love at first sight? No, but it was a whole lot of liking at first sight. (LOL)

I was a student at Hall High School and the only Black girl who had a white boyfriend. Byron treated all my girlfriends and me like queens. Byron attended college at night and worked full time during the day. He used his lunch break to pick me up from school. I didn't have to ride the school bus anymore! And if my friends were with me at school when it was time to go home, they got a chance to ride in the sports car also.

This is another important message for girls and women too. The man who is interested in you should be willing to make sacrifices for you. Byron sacrificed his time. He didn't want me to ride the school bus anymore when he could come and pick me up.

I would not recommend teenagers to marry so young. Enjoy your life, and if it's meant to be, it will happen. I say this because remember there was a six-year age gap for us (I was 16 and he was 22), and in most cases, not all females are mature enough for such an adult relationship. (I do understand that in some cases, females are more mature than the boy, but not in all cases.) I went from being a teenager to a young wife.

We dated and were soon married. This was 1974, and I didn't recognize the stares or mean looks that I'm sure we received. I was in love. I was always full of joy and energy, and that was part of what Byron says attracted him to me.

Early in our marriage, we had our first child. Nine years later, we had our second child. Again, my advice to teenagers is not to rush to get married or have children. Get your education and set some goals for your future.

I'm *old school,* so I still believe in no pre-marital sex or shacking (living with each other) before marriage. Take the time to get to know each other's families. This is so imperative. Know as much as you can about your boyfriend and his family. The Bible tells us not to be unequally yoked. I find that to mean having a misalignment of your goals. What about health? Is he clean, healthy, faithful, drug-free, etc.?

Knowing these things early on makes it easier to walk away from someone who you may be incompatible. It can be challenging to get out of a relationship that began too soon. Our feelings can outweigh our logic. Once you have sex and become intimate, it can be harder for a female to break it off if need be, because now you have feelings and believe you are in love. Some guys (NOT ALL) can cut their emotions off like a water fountain and move from one female to the next. In addition to abstinence, I suggest Godly counsel or wise professional counsel before getting into a serious relationship of any kind, especially marriage.

Is it hard to date outside your race?

In the seventies, there weren't many bi-racial couples, especially black females and white guys. White females with black guys were more prevalent. The former was rare, and a lot of times, it was kept a secret.

For me, it was not hard because we have so many nationalities within my family. Also, during my upbringing, my parents never used the N-word or talked poorly about other races. I was brought up in a Christian home and taught that everyone is equal.

Now my soulmate Byron's story is different. Byron came from Cairo, Illinois, and the residents there were, for the most part, not nice or friendly toward Black people. He witnessed riots, protests, and heard a lot of racist conversations in his home and at his school.

I'm always mindful of what the Bible says, "When a man finds a wife, he finds a good thing." (Proverbs 18:22)

So, my suggestion to my *Girl Power* readers, "Let the guy find you. You are a queen and should be respected, loved, and admired. Do not ever settle for less, and don't be anxious for anything. If he wants you, he will wait for you. Do not be afraid to talk to your parents or an adult about your relationship. Love feels good, it does not hurt and it is not one-sided.

No relationship is perfect. There will be good days and challenging days. They are called trials and tribulations. Healthy relationships should grow and get better.

Our marriage is what I call a marriage made in heaven. God selected us to be an example to show the world that two people from two different parts of the world, different races, and cultures could love and make it last. (46 years at the writing of this book)

It's 2020, and although we are living in unpredictable times, we recognize God as the head of our lives. Our love story started in 1974, and God is still leading us in 2020. So much has changed, but our love remains the same.

Time flies. I'm now 62, Byron is 67, and our children are grown. Our Daughter has blessed us with three amazing young adult grandchildren. Over these 40 plus years, we have learned so much together.

By the way, all the things I mention that girls and teens shouldn't do, I did it! But I learned from my mistakes and feel required to share with you what I know. My husband and I teach others the KEYS to having a happy, long-lasting friendship and marriage.

We frequently reminisce about the good old days when things weren't so expensive. Life was simple. There were no cell phones, computers were new, and there was no internet. Zoom. Facetime. What was that?

Although Byron and I were young and had a young family, education remained a priority.

This is where the village, tribe, family was so important. As a young family, we needed help. There were no books written on how to be the best parent. My mother and I are best friends, and she set a great example for me to mother my children. Although I never knew Byron's mother, something was done right because he turned out just fine.

I know that God kept us because more than 40 years later, we're still happily married. I, nor our children have ever met Byron's side of the family in person. We only spoke on the telephone and it wasn't pleasant. Unfortunately, they are the type of people who I spoke about early in my story who need to change their way of thinking.

Still, I salute and praise God, because if it hadn't been for Him being the head of our home, we couldn't have survived the open racism from the world nor the hidden racism from the other side of the family.

If God is for you, who can be against you!

What Has Happened Since 1974?

- President Richard Nixon resigned 1974
- Vietnam war ended 1975
- Margaret Thatcher, first woman elected to lead Britain's Conservative party 1975
- Egypt reopens Suez Canal after an eight-year war 1975
- I graduated from Hall High School 1976
- Jimmy Carter defeats incompetent Gerald Ford and became the first Candidate from the deep south 1976
- The Great Lakes Blizzard hits Buffalo New York 1977
- Roots television series, begins its phenomenally successful run on ABC 1977
- Jim Jones convinces 900 members of his church, *People's Temple* to commit suicide in Guyana 1978
- The Winter Olympics open in Lake Placid 1980
- The launch of the Hubble Space Telescope 1990
- Operation Desert Storm 1990
- Rodney King beating 1991
- The tearing down of the Berlin Wall 1991 (Iron Curtains)
- Oklahoma Bombing 1995
- Supreme Court of Florida orders a statewide manual recount of the votes in the presidential election 2000
- 911 Attack 2001
- Hurricane Katrina (The costliest hurricane) 2005
- The potential pandemic threat H5N1 - Bird Flu 2005
- Me Too Movement 2006
- Barack Obama - First African American/Biracial President 2008

- COVID-19 Pandemic 2020
- NBA legend Kobe Bryant (41) and his daughter Gianna (13) dies in a helicopter crash 2020
- Civil Rights Icon, Congressman John Lewis dies 2020
- Multiple Unjust Killings: Brenna Taylor, George Floyd, Ahmaud Arbery, Michael Brown, Terence Crutcher, Eric Garner, Oscar Grant, Freddie Cray, Botham Jean, Atatiana Jefferson, Bettle Jones, Trayvon Martin, Laquan McDonald, Tanir Rice, Dominique White.
- Girl Power and The New Normal 2020

The New Normal

Yes, we need to use our *Girl Power*.

How? Try to stay calm as much as possible. Invest in more downtime, rest, and find fun things in which to get involved.

Before you interact with someone (in person or virtual), remember the person(s) you're dealing with may not know these tactics, so you must set the atmosphere. Pray for your mental stability because things aren't the same as last year or the years past.

This is an excellent time to practice writing and sending 'love' notes to family members, friends, seniors, and neighbors. Take time to make phone calls to loved ones - it's even better if you can utilize FaceTime.

Girl Power Prayers: Pray for front line workers. They need proper protection gear: masks, gloves, face shields, hospital ventilators, and space for critical patients.

Pray for a cure!

Instead of in-person gatherings, we are moving towards drive-by celebrations to comply with social distancing requirements.

Restaurants are offering curbside options.

People are cooking more, growing gardens, and doing home renovations.

Schools are being encouraged to offer smaller classes while social distancing or virtual classes.

Churches are utilizing online options for worship.

Sadly, due to COVID-19, people are dying, losing jobs, and being evicted.

Divorce, suicide and domestic violence rates are increasing.

People are hurting, on edge, angry, and in need of solace.

How are you using your *Girl Power* to help create a New Normal that is positive, healthy, and productive?

Other areas impacted by COVID-19

Unemployment

Business Closings

Global Deaths

Technology Explosion (i.e., TikTok, Zoom)

Online Sells

Health Care Facilities Closing

Restrictions (Masks, Social Distancing): Nursing Homes, Gyms, Beauty Salons, Banks

In-Place Sheltering (cities, towns)

Live Television Shows/News Staff working from homes

Travel Bans

Food Pantries: Increased Need

Federal and State Facilities Close

Is There Anything Too Hard For God? No, God Has Us.

Girl Power

Suzette DeGaetano Charles (Born March 2, 1963)

American singer, entertainer, and actress

Miss America after Vanessa Williams forced to resign

Term: Miss America 1984 (seven weeks)

Titles Held: Miss New Jersey, 1983

Suzette is married to Ophthalmologist and Plastic Surgeon, Dr. Leonard Bley, and is the mother of two. She is biracial. Her father is Italian American, and her mother is African American.

Suzette was the first person of Italian descent to hold the title of Miss America. Following her short 7-week reign, she went on to have a career in entertainment. Currently, she enjoys life as a private citizen, wife, and mother.

Girl Power

Introducing Claudia Fountain ...

A unique situation. Sometimes God will design a particular time and season for people to meet, as nothing happens by chance. While conducting research and compiling a list of contributors for my book, *Girl Power*, it was vital for me to be sure to highlight a diverse group of women. Women of all backgrounds and nationalities make the world complete and would also complete my book.

As I moved forward, I began digging deeper into my family of Latinos. My family is comprised of many different races, so I started there first. It was incredibly challenging having to reach out to so many people. Everyone's lifestyle and schedules made it almost impossible.

Since I was working against a deadline, every moment was precious. So, I decided to solicit the help of friends.

My friend, Renee, seemed to have had a wide variety of contacts, and she shared a bit of Claudia's story.

When I finally connected with Claudia and she told me the rest of her story, I said, "This is the type of story that many people, especially young girls, would be moved by and most definitely glean from."

After reading her story, you will see why I had to include her in my book!

A Whole New World

Claudia Elisa Balderas Fountain

Living two worlds is not easy!

¡Viviendo dos mundos no es facil!

How can you live in two worlds and not lose yourself?

¿Como se puede vivir dos mundos sin perderte?

Two worlds. Two cultures!

¡Dos mundos dos culturas!

¡Welcome to my world!

Bienvenidos a mi mundo!

It was challenging for my family when they migrated from Mexico more than forty years ago in search of a better life. Unable to express themselves, to communicate, or to speak the language was very difficult.

Imagine living in a new and *totally* different culture than your own. Do you think you could handle it? Do you think you could adapt?

A whole new world of possibilities! "A fresh start at life in the United States," my cousins would say. "Are the streets paved of gold?" They would ask.

You see, I am the proud daughter of immigrants who believed America offered opportunities for success.

Girl Power: Claudia Fountain

I was born on July 20, 1972, in McAllen, Texas. It's also known as the Rio Grande Valley, which is north of the Mexican border. My late father, Roberto Arnulfo Balderas, was born on May 17th, 1933, in small-town called "Piedras Negras Coahuila." My father, a mixture of a renaissance man, a colorful storyteller, and a lover of poetry could name every Revolutionary War hero from both Mexico and the United States. Our father was an amazing provider and lover of God. He instilled in us that hard work, commitment, and dedication are the only way to get through life. He would also say that the only way you can make your dreams a reality is if you help someone else's dreams. Those are the words for which I live and die.

Then, there's my beautiful mother, Bertha Balderas Cienfuegos, born October 20, 1940, in Monterrey, Mexico. She's a classy lady with a mixture of fiery sassiness, a twist of firmness, and wit when it came to sales. Even with her limited English! My mom sold Avon for over 15 years and was top of her team. She also earned trips to Vegas and Florida as well as numerous awards for selling thousands of dollars' worth of Avon. What a boss lady!

My entrepreneur parents worked tirelessly to provide us with the best education and life. I am so grateful for them and the sacrifices they made for us! Parents always want better than what they had for their children. For them, it meant leaving their dream home in Monterrey, Mexico, more than 40 years ago.

I have two amazing brothers. My brother Roberto Balderas Cienfuegos was a criminal lawyer in Mexico and was raised by our grandmother. Unfortunately, he died a few years back from Parkinson's Disease. We miss him every day. Then, there is my overprotective, athletic brother, Gustavo Alejandro Balderas Cienfuegos. He is a hard worker and my father's assistant. Gustavo learned our family welding business at a young age and continued to work alongside my father for years until my father's passing.

Girl Power: Claudia Fountain

My beautiful sisters are three of the strongest women I know. Anna Luna is my prayer warrior. Lynda Nelly Cruz is my Cancer Survivor Warrior), and Patty, who has special needs but still managed to earn her High School Diploma. Patty has the sharpest memory of all!

Then, there is me - the youngest. I was the only one born in the United States. I was such a curious little girl with my head in the clouds, always daydreaming of being a successful educator one day. I was the wild one, the teacher's pet, the cheerleader, and the loudest one in my class!

My family made me feel like I had something extraordinary, almost like a "superpower" of some sort. But I was too young to understand what that was. Every day after school, my siblings would ask, "How do you say [this or that] in English?"

Haha! I used the experience of teaching them into an opportunity for me. I already loved to read, and now I had a chance to gain teaching techniques. My siblings got better at learning new words, and my love for teaching began! Learning to read is an essential part of everyday life. I started paying attention in school and would purposefully make friends with peers who didn't speak Spanish.

Can you imagine having to go to a school, and most of your peers don't speak your language?

As a little girl, my mother saw my enthusiasm and thirst for knowledge. She invested in a book club called Sweet Pickles. The books arrived monthly, and I quickly read them over and over. Later, I shared the importance of reading with my children. When we read, we are improving our memory and empathy. Your brain reacts as if you're *actually* living that experience. I just love how the mind creates intense, graphic mental simulations of sights, sounds, movements, and tastes they encounter in the narrative.

At the age of six, I was learning a new language! I watched American television shows such as Mr. Rogers, Sesame Street, and the infamous TV series, American Bandstand hosted by the legendary Dick Clark. (Don't act like you didn't watch these! Ha!) I would run to the *television se*t in our living room eager to watch these shows with my siblings and to try mimicking the dance moves of the American Bandstand dancers. What an incredible little magical world I created for myself!

As a young girl, I took the responsibility of teaching my family the English language because I did not want anyone to take advantage of them. Both my parents gave up so much to get to the United States. I felt I owed them that much to fulfill their dreams and make them proud!

March 10, 1997, I was 23 years old, sitting in a bowling alley on a Monday night filling out a flight attendant application when all of a sudden, the waitress brings me a margarita.

"From the gentlemen at the bar," she says.

I couldn't be bothered. I rejected it since I had just terminated a 5-year relationship only five months prior. All I wanted to do at this point was to explore all four corners of the world, even if it meant living out of my suitcase. The next thing I noticed were these enormous hands in front of me handing me a margarita.

"Would you rather have WOT-A?" He asked.

I'm like, "Come again?" When I tell you I was at a loss, I was nowhere to be found.

He repeated himself and asked, "Would you rather have a drink of water?" His accent was British. My knees got weak.

"Are you from Europe?" I asked and attempted to compose myself.

He said yes and that he was from Cambridge, England. We talked for several hours that night, and for weeks on and off until one day he asked me out on a date.

He was older than me, and all I could think about was how wrong it was. I could hear my mother's voice loud and clear, "¡Estas loca!" (You are crazy!)

I thought, *this man is 19 years my senior. He is too old!*

However, I was intrigued by his regal, educated, and cultured demeanor. He offered an opportunity for me to be exposed to the English culture, way of life, and living! It all sounded so exciting and refreshing.

Here I was a young 23-year-old Texan who was ambitious, goal-oriented, and a go-getter. I was ready to be whisked away to a new beginning.

Deep down, I knew that my parents would never accept this! But then again, I rationale, I was 23 years old. I was an adult and thought I knew best. I was ready to see what else life had in store for me. So, we went on our first date to a fancy dinner and a movie. He was so charming and charismatic; he knew how to treat a lady. Remember, I was only 23. I wasn't aware that all this 'courting' was his way of taking me away from my support group, my family.

Until then, the only constant in my life had been them, my beloved family. My family was old fashioned and traditional. We believed once you get married, you stay married. It's for life!

Girl Power: Claudia Fountain

My parents were married for 55 years. My siblings were with their spouses for 30 years.

Yes, I was vulnerable. I was the youngest daughter. My sisters were getting married, and this man sounded dreamy! So, I went for it! I took a leap of faith! I was in love and was whisked away to Arkansas to start a new life with this incredible new man didn't sound bad at all. We found a beautiful home in 1998 on Grandview Heights, where you could see the entire city. We created so many fond memories there. That's where I raised my children.

I applied for a job in Chinatown and was hired on the spot (Thank you, Mrs. Grace!). I worked there for a few years. Then, I found another job in Aramark at the University of Central Arkansas (UCA). I worked there from 2002-2006, and I later studied English Second Language (ESL) Specializing in Spanish. My long-life dream of becoming a teacher was finally becoming a reality. I spent four years waking up at 4:30 am to finish my homework while my family slept. There were so many sleepless nights trying to figure out how to maintain a grade point average of 3.5 throughout my four years of college.

Although the journey was amazing, times were tough. I didn't have any family here to help me with my two kids, who were 11 months apart. I had to hire a babysitter and keep going. I was working two jobs while maintaining a full-time status at school without any family support. They were all in Texas. For 21 years, I had a rocky marriage, but I was too busy to stop and get stressed about it!

Then, in 2004, doors began to open for me. I was honored to work under the supervision of Charlotte Green. As our principal, Ms. Green was an extraordinary visionary and leader. I was offered a position to teach Spanish at Focused Learning Academy, a first of its kind charter school in our city. I am proud to also share that I was the first Latina to teach Spanish to kindergarteners through 6th grade in my city. I was so eager to teach my students! I also created a Spanish club to further extend and share my culture. I'll never forget what one of my mentors would say when things got rough:

"Remember this, Claudia. We teach for the outcome, not for the income."

Things changed and luckily, I have always had multiples streams of income. (As you well know, a teachers' salary could benefit from an increase. That was true then and it is still true now. But I have faith in our educators, families, and community that this will change!

As for my marriage, all I ever wanted was to explore the world with a man guided by God, to love life, to have smart babies, and a cozy house to call my home. What I am about to share has never been said aloud. My story is every woman's fear. I thank my children, Joel and Victoria, for allowing me to share this delicate matter. It has been a difficult journey for us all.

Honestly, I was too embarrassed and proud to reach out to my friends and family about the toxic state of my relationship. My friends and family thought I was madly in love when really, I was under his constant wicked spell. I was in way too deep. My mind believed all the threats that were told to me, so I kept quiet for 21 years, until now! I was "powerless!" He had power and control over me! I was raised to be independent, and so for so long, I thought I was strong by tolerating his abuse. Our lives were his nightmare, not mine; I just happened to be the survivor.

My marriage was not easy. He knew how to love me in his own way, and as his wife, I accepted the challenge from the fallout of his cruel upbringing at the hands of his father. He shared with me about his demons. He told me that he and his father had an unhealthy relationship; at times, his dad would physically hurt him. That was his excuse for how he dealt with certain situations that he couldn't control. I, being a giver and protector, saw this as a challenge to help him heal, but his demons were far too much for my spirit to bear. I had to walk away from it all. The only one in control here was God Almighty. God had to intervene because it was up against a powerful demon. I continued to pray and continued to pretend I was ok! When in reality, I was broken!

I want to use this space to warn you that if the love you get from your spouse hurts, then it is not love! That is a toxic relationship, and you must get out NOW! There is help out there! Domestic violence comes on like a tsunami.

Hard facts: About one in four women will, at one point in their lives, be beaten or abused by someone they know. Four thousand women die because of domestic violence, and up to 75% of abused women who are murdered are killed after they leave their partners.

The first step toward recovering from any type of traumatic experience is re-establishing your sense of security and safety. Politically speaking, the systems in place to help were often just as oppressive as my abuser. We definitely need to level the playing field and get an education on how to listen to women in duress. I went to court, and it failed me. I had a stack of restraining orders, but law enforcement failed me. They did nothing! I took my determination to "stay alive" into my own hands. God has always led every step of the way!

I planned my getaway for six years. Yes, that's right, I spent six years setting aside money, confiding in best friends, and building allies. Christmas, December 2017, I knew in my head and heart that it would be the last one I'd spend in that house. I had rented a place and had nothing but a burning desire to move forward and finally have freedom from my past! I had never felt so much joy and pain at the same time: joy for finally picking up the pieces of a shattered life and agony over the possibility of resentment from my children. I was afraid they wouldn't understand since they never *saw* the abuse. But they *knew* that something was not right.

Pushing my doubts and fears aside, I took action!

I said **NO MORE** giving another second of my life to this marriage. It was not for me to fix this person. It would have to be his will to allow God to heal his heart and make the necessary changes!

I was only 24 years old when we had a son together, and a baby girl was soon on the way. He had me in my late twenties, all through my thirties, and almost through my forties. It was difficult, but I had to walk away from it all. I had to walk away from my husband. I had to walk away from my marriage. I had to walk away from my home, but not my children.

My love for my children was the force that kept me going. I had to sacrifice us to rescue us. My son wanted to stay with his father to support him emotionally, but my daughter decided to stay with me. I kept praying every day that one day we would, as a family, love ourselves even stronger in Jesus' name. We co-parent our children and have family dinners on Sundays. It's about the bigger picture. It's about forgiving for yourself and allowing things to heal and be transformed. We had to put our differences aside to create a healthy space for all of us to heal in our own way and still feel supported. Although my ex-husband and I are no longer together, he still is an amazing father and provider for our children.

God is the only way to salvation, and I prayed for so long that He would give me the strength to get out! This was such a paralyzing experience, kind of like being in a nightmare without the ability to wake up! You attempt to move your legs to run away, but you can't move. As the years went by, it became easier and easier to endure verbal abuse, physical abuse, and the resulting pain. There were times I wondered if people could see right through me. There came the point when I didn't care who knew anymore because I was exhausted. Hiding the agony and the pain began to wear me down.

There is a battle between the dark and the light. Choose the side of light by becoming more aware and not being a victim of your circumstances. At times, I still struggle. I will be honest; sometimes, my past gets the best of me. But I pray and remember that I've been delivered.

I forgave my ex-husband, and he knows I've forgiven him. Forgiveness didn't come easy. You ask, "Why me? Is there something wrong with me? What causes someone to do this to the brink of causing someone else harm?"

I realized he had never forgiven his father. So, the pattern continued. He became a product of his environment. I asked God to give me the strength and the courage to keep pushing through the pain. We are all created in His image and have the capability to love. I'm also aware that there is evil in this world, and people do harm intentionally. By the same token, we can also choose to love intentionally.

You may ask, "How does someone undo 20 years of darkness?"

By taking it one day at a time!

I am building a relationship with God. I am aware that in life, sometimes you must seek therapy so that you learn to trust again because it is a challenge for many. How do you heal from it all? I've learned that through forgiveness, you heal. It gives you the power to regain self-awareness, and that is one of the vital lessons in life, self-awareness of your strengths and weaknesses. I've learned to be around positive people whom I aspire to be like - entrepreneurs, spiritual leaders, self-employed business owners, and women in leadership roles. I think it's important to embrace those who are smarter than you so that you learn from them and take nuggets to build your own empire! I am proud that I have earned a colorful portfolio.

Encouraged from those nuggets, I continued to teach a diversity class at Magness Creek Elementary, law enforcement, local businesses, assisting special needs students, and investing in an import/export business class. Teaching was some of the best years of my life!

Pushing through the challenges, I reached a milestone. In 2018, I managed to hit six-figures! That was a huge accomplishment for me! I paid upfront for my daughter's senior trip for both of us to the Bahamas in 2018! That was also the first year, I humbly say, that with effort and sacrifice, I invested my time as well as my finances back into my community.

I love staying involved in my community. For me, money is a vehicle by which to sponsor certain non-profits that I support like *Arkansas United*, a non-profit that engages immigrant communities through outreach, education, training and information, and *CoHo,* who rebuilds families from within the lower socioeconomic neighborhoods. Just last year, on April 15, 2019, 133 families were going to be displaced, and we only had 60 days to work on the logistics. The landlord came to the grueling conclusion that he was in over his head with the rising costs of city water bills and could no longer adequately maintain the mobile home park. This was a very unique situation where the residents were predominately Hispanic and non-English speakers. When there is a tornado warning, you are prepared with lamps, shelters, emergency kits, etc. Well, not these families, they had been living there for over 20 years, and they had to go.

Can you imagine having to be uprooted against your will? We gathered our amazing local non-profits like *CoHo*, *Capca*, *Conway Ministries*, *Bethlehem*

House, *United Way*, and the *Salvation Army*. Then, there was me as a Spanish Interpreter collaborating with these amazing groups who serve our community on a daily basis. This trailer park had three months to pack up and go! Emotions were running high. We had 80 plus children and their parents needing to find housing quickly. We met every day for weeks and learned together along the way. It was a strenuous experience for all of us. I am happy to announce that everyone has found their new homes. I wouldn't trade these experiences for the world. It was one of the most fulfilling challenges of my life.

I had the honor to be the secretary for a non-profit called *League of United Latin American Citizens* (LULAC), which was founded in 1929. LULAC is the oldest and most widely respected Hispanic Civil Rights organization that advances the economic condition, educational attainment, political influence, housing health, and civil rights of the Hispanic population of the United States. We helped raise over $750,000 in scholarships over a period of 14 years through engaging the community and organizing Cinco de Mayo events in Little Rock, Arkansas. This is where my love for philanthropy ignited!

I am so proud of myself for making the decision to love myself more. That decision allowed me not only to nurture my children but gave me the courage to help others. When I wanted to throw in the towel, I reflected on my philanthropy work in the community and realized I had nothing to complain about. Others have no homes, no family, didn't wake-up, drug addictions, or were jobless. The human condition is remarkable and resilient! Just when you think you have it bad, someone out there has it worse! I always had to embrace my downfalls and continue to give to others to find my strength.

Even in the midst of your most desperate times, you can still give God all the glory. He sees your heart. Watch how He provides every time! Never give up because you may very well be the shift for a better tomorrow! Believing is achieving, and creating a happy life is your birthright!

It is not about what life throws at you, but rather how you react to the situation. Trust that God will walk with you. Ask yourself, "What is the most important thing in this world to me?"

My mental health was the most important thing for me, and I did everything I could to preserve.

It is 2020, the year for women to stand up and take charge of their lives fully: spiritually, mentally, emotionally, financially, and physically! There are no excuses, and we won't settle for less! Get ready for your new lifestyle change and allow yourself to feel that you deserve all the greatest things life has to offer. Never give anyone the power to say otherwise! Love yourself, quantify your life with knowledge, empower yourself every day, and stay humble. I hope my story added value and inspiration to your life. I implore you to peel back the layers of your life and find your pain. There lies your purpose! This was how I found mine!

You are unique! (*Tu eres unico!*)

There's no one like you! (*Nadie como tu!*)

You are POWERFUL!

You are REMARKABLE!

You are UNREPEATABLE!

Thank you! *(Gracias!)*

Latina Still Standing!

Girl Power

Kaliegh Garris (Born August 21, 2000)

Student

Miss Teen USA

Term: 2019

Additional Title(s) Held: American Model and Beauty Pageant Title Holder

---

Kaliegh Garris was born in New Haven, Connecticut. She is biracial (Her father is African American, and her mother is Caucasian.) and chose to wear her natural curls for the pageant. Prior to being crowned Miss teen USA, Garris was a dual-enrolled student at Joseph A Foran High School and the Educational Center for The Arts where she studies theater.

Introducing Paula McDore …

The incredible news came announcing Paula McDore as the 43rd Postmaster and the first African American female to hold this position.

As a die heart Arkansan, I love it when I hear about my sisters and brothers making history in the state.

I remember when I first met Paula. I believe it was when I ministered at her church for a women's program. She was referred to me via my Wellness Center and became one of my personal clients.

Paula is a very determined, dedicated, and powerful woman. She set goals and is very adamant about reaching them. She is also passionate about her church family and her beautiful daughter.

As her trainer, I watched Paula hold it all together. She expertly balanced family, church, career, and her *me-time*.

Paula understood the importance of investing in self-care, which included physical health as well as emotional and mental health.

Traveling was also included in her schedule.

Journey with me now as we learn more about Paula!

My Life: How It All Started

Paula Rena Hegler McDore

New Little Rock Postmaster Paula R. McDore takes her oath of office Wednesday from Arkansas District Manager Thomas O. Billington during a ceremony in the Capitol rotunda. McDore is Little Rock's 43rd postmaster and the first black woman to hold the position.

Before I begin, let me first say God is Faithful and to HIM be the Glory.

I was born and raised in Harrel, Arkansas, a small town located in southern Arkansas. Harrell is about four miles outside of the city of Hampton. Specifically, Summerville is the community in which I lived.

My father is the late Arthur Lee McCrae, and my mother is Dora Hegler. I was raised by my paternal grandparents, the late Booker, and Corene Cross. We lived in Milwaukee for a period of time until my grandfather retired from his job, and we moved back to Arkansas.

I had a good life growing up. Looking back, I think I thought we were not rich but not poor either. I certainly give credit to my mother (Corene) for being a good money manager and my Dad (Booker) for being a great provider. Life was comfortable from a kid's perspective. I'm a little tickled when I write this because it reminds me of a Facebook post where a parent was referencing her child being her little best friend who thinks she's rich! Little did I know that we were poor, just not as poor as others around us. I spent every summer in

Milwaukee with my cousins, and I can remember telling my Mom, "I'm moving to Milwaukee when I graduate from high school." They kept the house in Milwaukee with the intent that I would move back and would, therefore, have somewhere to live. Love changes things.

I am a 1989 Honor Graduate of Hampton High School. I graduated 10 in a class of more than 50. I have great memories of high school because we had fun! I was in all sorts of clubs from the BETA club and FHA to the Student Council and FBLA. I played the clarinet and was part of the marching band for a few years. I was also on the basketball team for a while. Looking back, high school was a blast. We certainly did not deal with the issues kids face today. There was no gun violence. If you wanted to fight, you met them at the stop sign. After a few weeks, things worked themselves out. We were conflict resolution solvers, a skill that is lost in this generation due to video games, texting, and minimal face to face social encounters. I loved my friends, and we thought we were the bomb.com.

I went to church every Sunday, and if someone was having an afternoon or an evening program, I went to that service. Many reading this will understand when I say I was required *(it wasn't an option)* to be in the choir, to be on the usher board, to participate and give themes, and to welcome and be the Mistress of Ceremonies for the Annual Youth Day Programs. By the time I graduated from high school, I was churched out. I rebelled against the church. I would go just not too often. However, about ten years later, I found myself longing for that relationship again.

Proverbs 22:6 says, "Train up a child in the way he should go: and when he is old, he will not depart from it." The foundation was laid. As a parent, I often wonder if I really gave my daughter that same foundation.

Does she really know her strength is in the Lord?

My prayer has always been that whatever she chooses in life; she will choose God first.

The church I attended with my sister-in-law did not feel like the place I needed to be. I expressed, to a friend, my need to find me a church home, and she suggested St Luke Baptist Church. I attended my first service, and by the 2nd visit, I found myself walking down the aisle. At this time, we were still in the *Red Building*. It was a big church with a small-town church feel. The people were very friendly. Mother McClendon, Mrs. Valerie, and Mrs. Lynette gave my baby so much love. I knew we were in the right place. I love my Pastor, Eric Alexander. He takes the time to get to know the new members, and he calls them by their name. It may seem like a small thing to some, but for me, it speaks volumes. I am not just another number. I'm at a place where everybody knows my name.

Love can make you do some crazy thangs (Yes, I said "thangs")! My every intention after graduation was to move back to Milwaukee to go to MATC and finally to go to Marquette University. None of which happened. I was in love and didn't want to leave my boyfriend. Wow! At the last minute, I decided to go to Southern Arkansas University Tech in Camden, Arkansas. I graduated in 1991 with an associate degree in Applied Science in Computer Programming. I worked at McDonald's when I was in school. After graduation, I could not find employment in my field. I became a certified nurse's assistant (CNA) and worked at a nursing home for a while. I got married, and after a couple of years, I moved to Milwaukee for about four months in 1994. When I moved back to Arkansas, we lived in North Little Rock. I had applied for several jobs, and I remember telling my Aunt that I had applied for a job with the Post Office. She made the statement that it could take years before I'd get a call. In March 1995, I began my career with the U.S. Postal Service.

Girl Power: Paula McDore

I started as a Transitional Employee (TE) Data Entry Clerk at the Sherwood Remote Encoding Center, known as the REC site. We keyed information from mail pieces that were unreadable for the machine. The machine, at another facility, would transmit an electronic image of handwritten mail, and we would key in the address information. This information would then be transmitted back to the processing plant to process the mail on automated equipment. We keyed mail for several facilities, including Dallas, North Texas, Shreveport, Fayetteville, and Little Rock. In 2000, I became an acting supervisor (204B) at the REC. In 2001, I was promoted to Supervisor, REC. In 2002, due to Optical Character Reader technology, REC sites across the country were closing. The Sherwood REC was closed in July 2002. I was RIF and decided to go back to school in order to maintain my employment with the postal service. I became a distribution clerk at the Little Rock Main Office. After about a month, I became an acting supervisor again. In January 2003, I entered the Associate Supervisor Program.

In April, I graduated and became a Supervisor, Customer Services. I worked at several stations in Little Rock, including Forest Park Station, Industrial Station, and Asher Station. In 2009, I was promoted to Manager, Customer Services at the Forest Park Station. In 2012, I was promoted to Manager, Customer Services at the Brady Station Post Office. In 2013, I became the 1st African American female in Arkansas to hold the position of Manager Post Office Operations. In this position, I was responsible for 84 offices in the Central Arkansas area, not including Little Rock and North Little Rock. In July 2015, I became the Postmaster of Benton, Arkansas. In September 2018, I became the 1st African American Postmaster of Little Rock, Arkansas.

Along with my permanent assignments, I've also held several detailed assignments, including Customer Service Operation Manager (Ft Worth, TX), Acting Safety Specialist, and OIC of Wrightsville, AR.

I want to say to everyone reading this, regardless of who you are, life will happen. You will experience highs and lows, both personally and professionally. How you deal with them will determine the outcome. When I started my journey with the Postal Service, I had no idea I would be where I am today. I will caution you to be mindful of the people God has placed in your life. Pay attention to those people who are always encouraging you to new levels. God always places people in your life to guide you in the direction of the path He has for you.

People will see in you what you may not see in yourself. Never shy away from the challenges, for they will make you better. Do not discount yourself based on where you come from. You are destined for greatness! It takes hard work, dedication, and giving more sometimes than what the paycheck calls for. I'm sure most of you have heard the phrase, "don't burn bridges!" This is so true, especially in the Postal Service, one day, you may be someone's boss, and within the next year, they may be your boss.

Every statement someone makes does not require a comeback. There will be bumps and bruises along the way; you must stay prayed up! I've held positions that have left me wondering, *why me?* In hindsight, I now know there was a reason I was placed in those positions. It was all in preparation for what was and is to come. Preparation is needed so you can be ready and successful in the new position.

I often tell people who are looking to get into management; you must first be good at the position you were hired to do. People are always watching and taking notes. Regardless of what position you hold, remember you are needed and add value to the company. As I have matured in life, I now understand people are my greatest assets. It takes all of us to make it work every single day.

Nia Imani Franklin (Born July 27, 1993)

American Composer and Beauty Pageant Title Holder

Miss America

Term: 2019

Additional Title(s) Held: Miss New York 2018

Nia Imani Franklin was crowned Miss America Atlantic City, New Jersey. As a winner, she was awarded a $50,000 scholarship and will earn a six-figure salary during her reign.

Girl Power

Introducing Stacy Moultrie ...

Girl Power isn't always pink and frilly. I met Stacy Moultrie over ten years ago. She came to me needing help. Stacy was having some health challenges with a knee injury. She said my Wellness Center was highly recommended to her. Her former Taekwondo instructor had been a client of mine; the program was a success for him. I noticed how determined she was to get her body back into physical condition. There wasn't any activity I asked her to do that she didn't give me 100 percent. I was amazed by her physical strength and stamina.

At one time, I had an opportunity to see her Taekwondo skills put to the test. That sold me. This young lady was able to teach what she was trying to do again. So, I decided to invite her to a girl's summer camp that I directed. She was asked to come and demonstrate her skills, and the rest is history. All the girls and staff were amazed by her ability to execute her talents.

She continued to train under my guidance and reached the goals she had set for herself. So, when it was announced on the 5:00 pm news of her accomplishment of being the first female football official to do a state playoff game in Arkansas, I wasn't surprised.

I think I was more excited for her than other Arkansans when they heard the news. After reading her story, I think you will be too!

My Story. My Stingers. My Success.

Stacy Moultrie

The Early Years

You don't realize until you get older and go through somethings in life, how blessed you really are. To this day, I do not take anything in life for granted. Waking up in the morning or lying down at night is a blessing.

At the age of seven, I remember my grandparents coming to get my brother and me from Michigan to move back to Little Rock. Charles and Rosemary White raised us from that day forward. We were fortunate enough for them to come and get us and to take us under their wings. I won't go into details of my life in Michigan, but let's just say it was rough for a while.

My grandparents were the best parents anyone could have ever had. They were married for 58 years, and all the days of my life living with them, I never saw them argue, fight, or have anything disruptive between the two of them. My grandfather worked for 53 years at the University of Arkansas in Medical Sciences, where he began his career as a child psychologist and ended it as Vice Chancellor of Human Relations. My grandmother taught English and French in public schools for all her professional career. They were dedicated to their lives and family, as well as their careers. Their marriage and humbleness, as well as their longevity in their jobs, inspired me throughout my teenage and college years. They were always there for my brother and I as well as other family members and friends.

"No" or "I can't" weren't really words in our vocabulary.

My grandfather was a big sports enthusiast which is what got me into loving sports. He played golf, coached my brother's little league teams, and also the women's softball team at his job. I traveled everywhere with him to every game.

Watching the love that my folks had inspired me to want to give back. I learned to work hard for what I wanted. Even though I really didn't have to work while in school, I wanted to make my own money. My first few jobs as a teenager were waitressing at the Arkansas Arts Center and babysitting because of the love that I had for children. Once I turned 18-years-old, I applied to be a Big Sister with Big Brothers/Big Sisters of Pulaski County. To this day, I have been a member with them and have had a little sister ever since. I have had four little sisters whom I have seen all graduate high school. My present little sister is in the ninth grade right now.

The Educational Years

I attended Hendrix college for my undergraduate studies with the anticipation of going to Medical School. In my third year at Hendrix, I applied to and was accepted to the Medical Technology School at the University of Arkansas for Medical Sciences (UAMS). While in Medical Technology School, I worked as a lab assistant in the blood bank. Once I graduated, I started working at UAMS as a Medical Technologist. I loved it so much that I stayed in that position for twelve years. I developed a fondness for computers. So much so that I went back to school at UALR and earned a degree in Information Technology. Once I finished that degree, I was blessed to have an opening to support the blood bank system at UAMS. I was hired as a Clinical Systems Analyst in 2000 and worked in that position until 2018. While working as a Clinical Systems Analyst, I pursued my master's in information technology at Phoenix University. In 2018, I was offered a job at Wellsky, formally known as Medicare Information Systems, where I am presently working remotely as Senior Computer Systems Analyst. I have worked for thirty years at UAMS. Never would I have imagined working in one place for that long. I guess I got that from my grandparents.

The Dramatic Life Changes

As I mentioned before, I was really blessed to have the best grandparents ever. I never really had to ask for much and didn't take them for granted. I had a chance in my life to make a move to Texas for a job offer, but I couldn't imagine leaving my grandparents as they were up in age and needed help. So, I decided to stay put. They had done so much for me in my life. I wanted to stay around and take care of them. My brother and his girls were in Atlanta, Georgia, and my Dad lived in Mississippi. He later moved to Georgia also.

At twenty-nine, a dramatic change happened. It really opened my eyes and showed me to never take anything in life for granted. I don't talk about it much, but this year was one of the hardest years of my life. I was pregnant. In my ninth month, my grandfather had a stroke and was going to have to have triple bypass heart surgery. My grandmother was the stronghold and was there for my papa. While my papa was in the hospital, I went for my ninth month checkup. I was by myself, and during the checkup, my doctor told me that I needed to go to the hospital next door. He said he would meet me over there. When I got there, the doctor told me that my child was stillborn. This was one of the most devastating times in my life. I still had to deliver my child. As you can imagine, my papa's surgery and the birth of my stillborn child caused an enormous amount of stress. As I was healing from that, I learned why they say things come in threes. Six months later, the father of my child was killed in a car accident, and six months after that, his son from a previous marriage drowned on July 4th. To say the least, that year was a trying year, but the Lord took me through.

I am telling my story to tell those who read this that life is not always going to be great. The Lord took me through tests and trials as He does with everyone. Tests and trials come in different ways, and we all handle things differently. Going through all of this taught me more and more about how precious life really is.

I tore my ACL, MCL, and Mencius. Besides being mad about not being able to compete, I was upset because I was not able to keep my workouts going. I had gotten into great shape and was ready to compete. When I had my surgery, the doctor told me not to be alarmed about how much my leg was going to be *mushy,* as you would say. Unable to work out for about ten months, I ended up picking up an extra fifteen pounds I didn't want.

After I was released from physical therapy and was approved to work out, I heard about Mrs. Phyllis Hodges, the Carousel Fit 4 Life, and all the successful clients she had. I went to check her out. I went for a trial six-week program. I had always worked out, but it's good sometimes to have someone else push you and give you an incentive in a different way. I weighed in at 185 pounds. Ugh!

It took at least three weeks to start seeing progress with the way my body loses weight. But I can remember I lost at least 10-13 inches in the two weeks before I started to lose weight. Combined with exercise, meal plans, massages, and prayer, Phyl got me rolling. I ended up losing weight and got down to 149 pounds. I was back to running like I was before. I feel better these days than I felt in my college years.

Phyllis was amazing, and the program was great. The days I didn't feel like working out, she pushed me. I also had a tear where my sciatic nerve hit me two years ago. I thought it was just back pain at first. But then it migrated down my right leg all the way to my foot. I endured numbness for three months. I was scared I wasn't going to get over this. This was more excruciating than my knee injury and surgery. I started doing physical therapy, and the therapist mentioned that massages could help work the knots out. Well, I put in a call to Mrs. Phyl again. She worked wonders on my back and leg. It was excruciating at first, but it helped get me going again. If you ever have sciatic problems, I recommend massages from Phyl if you can get her. (Smile)

To this day, I try to get in at least four to five days of some kind of workout. It's great for the mind, body, and soul.

Organization

Not that I didn't know before, but tragedy and loss taught me firsthand to never take life for granted and to cherish every waking day the Lord gives you.

After going through that tough year, I tried to go to therapy sessions, but it just wasn't for me. It made it harder for me and was depressing, so I instead just kept myself busy. I returned to work, kept myself busy in church, and continued spending time with my little sister from Big Brothers/ Little Sisters. The mother of my little sister knew what I had been through and asked me, later on, if I would like to become a foster parent.

I decided to take a stab at it. The first child I welcomed into my home was a three-year-old girl. She stayed in my home for three years before being moved to another home. The next child I fostered was a little boy. He was three as well, and two weeks later, they asked if I could take another child. This was another little boy, but he was only five weeks old.

I was like, "Wow. What are you doing? No kids of your own and taking on others?"

Well, the two boys ended up being in my home for two years. I contemplated adopting the baby boy and started looking into it. I felt bad about keeping him and not the older one. So, long story short, I ended up adopting both.

Again, I asked myself, "What are you doing tying yourself down with children when you don't have to?"

God always has a plan.

Well, I had plenty of help, as it takes a village. My grandparents, family, friends, church family, motorcycle family, and Taekwondo family all pitched in to help me raise these little boys who would have a lot of issues ahead of them. While working full time, doing my extracurricular activities, and spending time with family, I still managed to have time for the boys too. There were some trying times with the boys as they both had more issues than normal children do. The older child dealt with coming from a family of siblings and not being able to be with them. The younger one was diagnosed with ADHD and Bipolar Disorder, which came from birth.

The next seventeen years of my life were trying with them. But with the help of family and friends, I managed. I decided that if I were going to have any more kids, it would be if I were married. For these two, I made sure they stayed in church, sports, and activities. While taking them to football and basketball practices, I met some great friends. Some of which were referees.

The Refereeing Years

And that is how I got into the world of refereeing. The boys' football coach kept saying, "Come on, let me make you one of the first female football referees in Arkansas."

I was like, "Really?" and then after some thought, I said, "Well, I guess I could try it."

I started out with youth leagues in football and basketball, in boys' and girls' clubs, and tournaments. After a few years, I worked my way up to high school games. I joined the Arkansas Officials Association and began refereeing football and basketball games all across Arkansas. I attended camps and clinics throughout the summer to enhance my skills and learning. The first couple of years of football were tough, mostly due to coaches who didn't like change or want to see a female on the football field. I realized I had to get some tough skin if I wanted to stick with it, which is what I gained. After a while, when I started throwing my flag, and they realized that I wasn't going to put up with too much, I gained respect.

The primary position in which I work is head linesman (working the chains), but I have worked every position on the football field. I found my way on a crew and have been on that crew for the last fifteen or so years. I have made some great friends because of it.

Girl Power: Stacy Moultrie

For the last seven or eight years, I have been the white hat (the referee) in some Friday night games. With basketball, it wasn't as hard because females were known more to referee this sport. While it wasn't as hard, you still had to gain respect with and develop a thick skin. I have been doing football and basketball for over twenty-five years now. I worked my way up to doing D2 women's college basketball and the rest of the sports high school and below. I referee football, basketball, softball, volleyball, and little league baseball. In 2016, I received a call to see if I was available to do a first-round football playoff game.

I didn't think twice and said, "Sure."

He was like, "You will make history in Arkansas by being the first female to do one."

I was like, "Wow, that's cool."

One of the moments I'll never forget about was this game was in November. It was mild, still cold to me. I arrived at the game and prepared to get dressed. I put on long sleeve undergarments and a long sleeve shirt. I came out, and I saw all the guys had on short sleeve shirts.

"Hey guys," I said, "it's cold outside."

"Oh no, it's not," they said. "We are wearing short sleeves."

That meant I had to do the same. I was mad, but since we had to be dressed alike, I had to go change. To say the least, I was cold the whole game and nervous too. I don't know why I was nervous because it was just another football game. I think the nerves were overworking with four guys whom I had never worked with before. They all knew each other, and here I was walking in as a female doing a playoff game with them.

I was working the linesman position that night.

It didn't take long to see that a couple of my partners didn't trust my judgment and calls. About halfway through the first quarter, we had a couple of plays to my side.

The white hat ran over to my side and asked, "Did you see that?"

"No," I said. I was thinking to myself, *really*?

A couple of plays later, I called holding, and the umpire had the same flag as me.

The white hat ran over to me again and asked, "You sure?"

I was like, "Are you serious?"

I thought to myself, *come half time I will address this.* The white hat seemed like he didn't trust that I knew what I was doing. At halftime, I was getting ready to say something, but the umpire beat me to it. This was funny to me.

He said to the other guys, "Listen, I am sure if she didn't know what she was doing, she wouldn't have gotten picked to do this playoff game."

I was like, *ok, I guess I don't have to say anything now*. To say the least, the second half was better for me. I made it through, and it was a good experience.

I would say to any referee of any sport, "You have to love the game to want to do it."

It's not just about the money. Don't get me wrong, the money is good, but if it's not a career for you, you have to be willing to deal with coaches, players, fans, and even other referees.

If you want to be a great referee, you have to also be willing to put in the time to go to camps and clinics to keep learning. No matter how long you are in the game, you will always see and learn something new.

I plan on refereeing as long as the Lord allows.

The Extracurricular Activities

Even with a full-time job, two children, and a dog, I still manage to have extracurricular activities. I am very involved with my church. I was a youth choir director for a while. I sing in the choir, and I'm on the praise team. I took Taekwondo as a child and just happened to get back into it for a second time in 1998. I practiced it until 2008. It was a great stress reliever. It also helped to get me in shape. I started competing in tournaments most weekends and training three to four times a week. I was even at the top of my league in sparring for my age group for a good while.

In 2003, I pursued becoming a Taekwondo school owner.

After taking a few business classes and doing research on entrepreneurship, I applied for my business license and was granted a license from the American Taekwondo Association in 2003. I opened my school (Moultrie's ATA) in 2003 and had some success for a while.

One night I was practicing for my fourth-degree black belt while also competing for the top in sparring at my school. I was at the top of my game at this time. One of the tests I had to do was to jump over a chair and break two boards with a sidekick. Well, after numerous jumps, I came down on my knee, and it buckled. I thought I had just sprained it. I went home that Friday, and using my medical field thinking, I decided just to ice it, soak it, and heat it. I thought it would be better by Monday. Well come Monday, I was at the doctor's office and was sent to orthopedics. I found out I had torn my ACL, MCL, and meniscus. I was distraught. I was at the top, physically and mentally. Now I wouldn't get to test for my fourth degree or be able to compete for the World Championships that June. The doctor told me he had the same tears from skiing.

"If you want to be able to run and referee again, you will have to have surgery."

So, there wasn't a second thought about it; I would have to have it. I tore my knee in June and was scheduled for surgery in September. Afterward, the doctor scheduled me for physical therapy.

Talk about excruciating pain! But I had the best physical therapist. It turned out that he was in Jujitsu himself. So, I told him about another testing in April and asked if it was possible for me to be ready for it. He said it was possible. He worked me over and over. He even added in some extra exercises like my martial arts kicks to get me ready.

The other patients in the room were like, "We don't have to do that do we?" (smile)

He had me running in three months, and that April, I was able to test for and pass my fourth-degree black belt testing.

Sadly, the doctor did advise me that I might want to give up Taekwondo if I didn't want to reinjure my knee or hurt the other one. The pounding, twisting, and turning was putting a beating on my knees.

So, as much as I loved Taekwondo, I had to give it up, especially if I wanted to continue to referee.

I closed my school in 2008. It was nice while it lasted.

I still offer self-defense classes sometimes for churches or other organizations. I was also certified in ground fighting, kickboxing, knife self-defense, and a few other martial arts.

As I mentioned before, I am a Big Sister with Big Brothers/Big sisters of Pulaski County and have been since I was eighteen years old. I was voted Best Sister in 2017.

I also ride motorcycles and have been a part of the Real Rock Ryders Motorcycle club since 2003.

As you can tell, whatever I take part in, I give it my all and stick with it for a long time.

One of my most dreamed about accomplishments was becoming a part of the greatest organization, Delta Sigma Theta Incorporation, and carrying on the legacy of my grandmother. In Spring 2018, I was able to cross the burning sands and become a part of the Little Rock Alumnae Chapter of Delta Sigma Theta Inc. I had dreamed about this since my undergraduate college years, but I didn't try at the time because of school and the kids. I loved the sisterhood, giving back to the community, and gaining fifty-two of the best sisters on my line as well as across the country. I know my grandmother is looking down on me, smiling from ear to ear.

I am telling my story to tell everyone this: "It's not about the obstacles around you, but how you jump over and get around those obstacles. Life takes you through tests and trials that the Lord will see you through."

I heard a pastor say, "A bee can sting you once, but once you're stung that one time, it can't sting you again."

Toni Ann Singh (Born February 1, 1996)

Model, Blogger

Miss World

Term: 2019

Additional Title(s) Held: Previously Crowned Miss Jamaica World

---

There have been four Miss World titles awarded. Toni- Ann Singh of Jamaica, was the fourth. Toni-Ann Singh was crowned on Dec. 14, 2019, in London, England. The 23-year-old Psychology graduated of Florida State University in Tallahassee with a degree in women's studies and psychology.

Toni was born in Jamaica Morant Bay, she came to the US at the age of nine and settled in Florida.

Introducing Dr. Georgianne Thomas ...

In the process of interviewing and researching for "Girl Power," I find myself reminiscing about what it means to have and reflect female influence. This is a most rewarding gift God has birthed inside of me.

I thought, "Who do I know? Who have I read about? What women have a testimony and a rewarding story that could help change the lives of our youth and other females?

I wanted someone who was a part of history, whom most folks wouldn't know about but should. I decided to call my friend, the cover designer for my last book and this one, artist Laurence Walden (aka Blinky) for direction. Of course, he knows everybody. I laugh and say, "Blinky knows the haves and the have nots." (LOL)

Blinky told me about a lady whom I had never heard of. Then, he began to share with me about a special project that he was working on with her. I stopped him in the middle of the phone conversation and said, "She is the one. People need to know this history!"

Within 48 hours, she called me, and it was like we have known each other all our lives.

I can't wait for you to read about Dr. Georgianne Thomas.

Life After Seventy

Dr. Georgianne Thomas

"The years of our life are seventy, or even by reason of strength eighty; yet their span is but toil and trouble; they are soon gone, and we fly away." **Psalm 90:10 ESV**

On August 1, 2012, the night before my birthday, I could barely sleep. My daughter, Reverend Alvelyn Sanders, could feel my excitement. She asked me if I wanted to do something special. Deep down inside, I wanted a party, a celebration, and a fete, but the fear of not crossing into God's promised land made me just want to sit and wait for midnight.

Secretly, I cried because I certainly did not feel worthy of reaching the number seventy. I reflected on the number of incidents in my life for which I was not proud. I remembered the very painful times of my youth too shameful to disclose. I pondered over the fact that I had lived through three marriages by age forty-five.

Mirror, Mirror, on the Wall, who the heck is this person?

Painstakingly, I examined my present state (age seventy) and marveled at God's grace for allowing midnight to come so that joy could meet me in the morning. I was turning seventy. At this pivotal point in my life, accomplishments did not matter. I managed to do something pleasing to God between the turmoil, turbulence, and trouble of my life. He had heard my cry. My cup runneth over. Grace and Mercy were still with me. All I could think about was my grandmothers' prayers that had followed me from birth to August 1, 2012, and midnight was quickly approaching. August 2nd was approaching its dawn.

How did this little girl get from Gary, Indiana, earn a doctorate, raise an accomplished daughter with three Masters degrees, teach a multitude of youth all scattered throughout the universe, survive breast cancer, and most recently, colon cancer? How did so many missed opportunities still yield a full life of fun, frolic, freedom, and a fear of the Lord? How did it yield an iconic life after so many disappointing, failed endeavors, businesses, music and entertainment, marriages, health, wealth, and personal love and growth?

Only God. It was His Will that ushered in my proud title: **SEPTUAGENARIAN**. What a Blessing. Midnight arrived. August 2, 2012 was a new day dawning on a new adventure called life.

Now, I am seventy-seven going on fifty-seven, and I'm glad to have reached a point in my life where time and age do not exist. Yes, I share the septuagenarian universal aches and pains. My body sends messages to my brain as gentle reminders of my longevity. I have chosen, however, to repackage those messages, to send them back to my brain, and to receive new extended energy. My brain then receives a younger message and reacts accordingly. I have attempted to share these ideas with many of my fellow seniors, only to be met with the standard chorus line, "**I AM TOO OLD**."

Well, this song does not work in the matrix where I have chosen to live and still grow. I did not arrive at this marvelous state by myself, but with the help of one of my elder students who returned to college to receive his Bachelor of Science degree at age 60. He introduced me to myself through a series of motivational videos and books of enlightenment relevant to erasing age and time from my matrix. Once I reengaged with myself, I liked myself much better. There was also another genius student who joined in the quest to awaken the other Georgianne. Together, they took me to the woodshed and gave me an *intellectual, third-eye, wake-up call, whipping*. Oh, my goodness, I can still feel the sting of the whip of knowledge from the Moses Code, Indigo Elder, The Secret, The Emerald Tablets, Numerology, the Pineal Gland, and more.

Cornell Pearson and Shon Walker awoke in me a sleeping giant. I revisited the projects I had put under the bed, in the drawer, and in the snooze locker of my mind. I was introduced to younger people who were glad to know me and wanted to spend time enjoying my company. I became more technologically savvy, which opened the world, not just a highway. I always had a penchant for technology, so this was my easiest transition.

The most difficult transition to my matrix was to stave off the time-capturing me that was in a capsule and would send me to my grave, unfulfilled and flat-out disappointed. There was still life to live, and since there was no age and time in my matrix, I needed to get on with my new extended, vibrant, spiritually grounded life. I had more things to do, new people to meet, more books to read, more kisses to give, and more life to live.

Just knowing there were more people like the new me was fascinating. I am not declaring a **WONDER WOMAN** status. However, I declare Georgianne is a wonder woman in a humbling way because she knows and has seen the power of prayer in her life now more than ever. Breast cancer, seventeen years ago (healed), and colon cancer 2019 (healed) battled with chemotherapy daily for six months. In my matrix, another Georgianne was created. Perhaps this Georgianne is the one who raised her hand and asked to come to earth. Maybe it took her this long to revisit her assignment but with new fervor and new energy! This is **GIRL POWER** at seventy-seven, full of life, energy, and fun. I continue to create projects and revisit old ones. I am all about the business of finishing all of them.

How did it all begin?

Gary, Indiana, 1942. Growing up in Gary was like any other northern, small industrial town. It had four distinctive seasons, winter being more pronounced. We experienced all the usual *American Pie* kind of lifestyle. My mother and father divorced. My mother remarried and had two children, my siblings, a brother, Vincent Young, and a sister, Paquita Young. We had Sunday dinners. We attended both the White Sox and Cubs games. We had an active church life. We attended elementary, junior high, and high school. We laughed and played. We shopped in Chicago and visited all of the Field Museums, the Aquarium, and the Planetarium on Lake Shore Drive, Chicago. We went to the beach, had picnics, and played tennis and golf. Life was normal for the Young household. It was an easy lifestyle because Chicago and Gary were about twenty-five minutes away. By the time I was eight years old, I was traveling the South Shore Train system by myself to Chicago to meet my real Dad. By twelve, I was riding the Chicago El by myself. Who knew this independence was shaping me to be the person I am today? Fearless, independent, and my own woman.

After Spelman College and after a master's degree from Georgia State, I had some major challenges in life, including raising a daughter alone after a divorce. I even had a rock bottom experience, but that never stopped me from reaching for the stars, and knowing in my mind, I would touch them. Failing was never an option.

The wake-up call that really set the tone for who I am today was when I stepped off the train in Atlanta, Georgia, 1960, and saw the signage that said

Colored Waiting Room and White Waiting Room. My parents had sheltered me from the reality of being Black in America and especially Chicago.

What was a Colored Waiting Room?

I decided to go to the White Waiting Room. I had no fear because I had lived in a mixed-race neighborhood. My school was mixed. My teachers were predominately White, and my stepfather said we were Americans, and we had to always honor the flag.

I heard a voice call my name as I was approaching the White Waiting Room. It was the voice of the young woman from Spelman who had been assigned to meet new students at the train, bus, or airplane terminals.

"Georgianne," she said, "you cannot go in there."

"Why?" I asked.

Her look said, "Get in the Jitney (I did not know we were not in a taxi) and let us go to campus." Then she instructed the driver, "Spelman College, Atlanta, Georgia."

The rest of this story is history. On October 19, 1960, after a series of classes and rallies on non-violence for the new Civil Rights Movement, I joined this movement with my fellow students from Spelman College, Morehouse College, Clark College (before the merger with Atlanta University), Atlanta University, Morris Brown College, and the Interdenominational Theological Center, in the largest coordinated, series of Civil Rights protests in Atlanta's history as college freshmen. It was the march that changed the world. It was the march that changed my life. I was burned with a cigarette from a White man who jumped in front of me as we picketed in front of Rich's Department Store. By then, I had become used to the jeers, the name-calling, the N-word, and being spat upon, but this act was memorable and impressed my freshmen mind: I was hated because of the color of my skin. These people did not know me. They did not know I had gone to schools with Whites, lived in the same neighborhoods with Whites, and had White friends.

Traveling back and forth to school from Gary to Atlanta for four years (1960-1964), helped me see clearly the racial prejudice in the North and the South. It showed me being smart, well-read, well-spoken, and well-traveled had no impact on White Americans who were prejudiced against Black people, period. I shut down all White people and interacted with them on an *as-needed* basis. My world as I knew it was shattered but for a good reason. The truth would set ME free, and I was truly free to be a Black woman, with no apologies!

I was the first Black person to work in Public Relations at Delta Air Lines, Inc. (1979). I was grateful to be working full-time after leaving the teaching community and my second divorce. However, there were and still are many challenges to being the first Black anywhere in Corporate America. Trust me; I had my share of issues in this position. I survived because they moved me out of the department. I am happy to say I am a Delta Air Lines, Inc. retiree. I do not know how I landed where I landed, but I thank God for retiring from Delta's Training Department.

I am so grateful to many co-workers such as Sandra East Jackson and Bruce Wayne McMillan for taking time to pour not only their personal resources into helping me raise my daughter, but they and many others encouraged me with super acts of kindness (Frances, Linda, and Rowene) to fight the fight and stay on the journey until my daughter graduated from college (Northwestern University). I retired at age fifty-two.

There was a lot of life between fifty-two and seventy-seven. The many heartbreaks, heartaches, and financial battles were just what I needed to fail and get right back up. I am now an Adjunct Professor at Clark Atlanta University.

I am working on my music and my dad's Big Band Music from the forties and fifties. I have two lines of greeting cards, two books, and a line of skincare products all waiting in the wings.

My daughter wrote, produced, and directed an award-winning movie named "Foot Soldiers: Class of 1964" (IMDb). I have been an extra in nineteen movies, featured on OWN, "BLACK WOMEN OWN THE CONVERSATION," and in numerous radio, television, and newspaper articles about the movie, "Foot Soldiers: Class of 1964," where I was the Executive Producer.

I'm not getting any older. I'm getting younger. My mantra for life's kicks and bruises is, "Once you shut yourself down with **I AM OLD**, you shut down the brainpower, the spirit, the soul."

Stop it!

There are still some books, some music, and some songs in your life. There are some elections still to be won, some love to be found, and a kiss to be received.

GIRL POWER is finding your voice, calling your name, believing in God, and not ever being ashamed.

Thank you for wanting to know about life after seventy. Some of us are still living!

Then the Lord said, *"My Spirit shall not abide in man forever, for he is flesh: his days shall be 120 years." Genesis 6:3 (ESV)*

Girl Power

Zozibini Tunzi (Born September 18, 1993)

South African Model and Beauty Queen

Miss Universe

Term: 2019

Previous Title(s) Held: Miss South Africa, 2019

Zozibini Tunzi, age 26, is the third woman from South Africa to win the title.

Introducing Helaine Raye Palmer Williams ...

I asked this professional, passionate, powerful woman of influence to be a part of my *Girl Power* book because, as a writer for *The Arkansas Democrat-Gazette*, she is well known and beloved. During a time when there weren't many faces of color appearing regularly in the newspaper, Helaine's face appeared weekly. Helaine's articles were always intriguing, thought-provoking, and amusing. I would always say, "This writer isn't just a writer; she's an anointed writer."

Time went by, and as providence would have it, we found ourselves in some of the same social and Christian circles and became friends. Helaine loved fashion, and at the time, I modeled and owned a modeling agency, *Ms. Phyl and Co*. We would also find ourselves serving as co-emcees for various events.

Then, one day, Helaine joined my Wellness Center. Always transparent, she wrote about her work out experiences as well as her updated eating habits. She wrote the good, the bad, and the ugly! Reading her newspaper articles was like reading a good book. Each week, I eagerly awaited Helaine's articles because they showcased people like me – people of color who were interested in fashion, entrepreneurship, charities, education, politics, and health.

Helaine's work is reminiscent of that of Mr. John Johnson (Ebony and Jet Magazines). Once, Mr. Johnson's work was the only avenue of advertisement for African Americans. Today, we can also credit Helaine Williams with providing exposure for our businesses and services. Read more about Helaine!

An Answer to a Prayer

Helaine Raye Palmer Williams

I like to tell people, "I was the answer to a prayer." Unable to help myself, I usually add, "So be careful what you pray for!"

But really, I was an answer to a prayer. My mother, an African American Army wife who already had three sons and four stepdaughters, wanted a daughter "of her own." Knowing that Hannah, the barren woman in the Holy Bible (Samuel 1), hadn't done too shabby by asking God for a child, she prayed to give birth to that daughter. Mama told me the story of how she and Uncle Tim, her next-to-youngest brother, were out for a drive in 1956 and were listening to an old radio show, "The Shadow." The particular episode to which they were listening featured a female character named Helaine.

"What a pretty name," Mama told Uncle Tim. "If I have a daughter, I'm going to give her this name."

I came along six years later at the Army hospital at Fort Leonard Wood, Missouri. And as they say, the rest is history. I was the youngest of a blended family of eight children.

When I was six, however, my parents parted ways. There were six of us still living at home. My mother packed us up, left Rolla, Missouri, and brought us to her birthplace of Little Rock, AR.

My mother was an avid reader, and soon I became one, too. Yes, I dutifully read the elementary-school reading books that told of the exploits of Jack, Janet, and their pets, Tip and Mitten. But soon, I was reading my mother's books. These books became my mode of traveling, of seeing the world. While I scoured the school library, ordered children's books through the mail-order service available at school, and bought every Trixie Belden mystery I could find at the store; I was also reading adult mysteries and romances.

In some respects, I was a sheltered child. Mama kept me close, raising me to believe I deserved the best in life. I apparently inherited her tendency to take mental excursions from the hassles of life and daydream about having and doing things on a grand scale. This was a tendency nourished by those books I read.

Until I was six years old, I was skinny, fairly happy, and fairly confident, insulated from the issues that not only ended my parents' marriage but also adversely affected my older siblings' quality of life. When my parents separated, and we moved, I experienced what I now realize was culture shock. I went from an environment that was predominantly white to a black rural neighborhood full of children I didn't act or talk like. We went from indoor plumbing and running water to a world of chamber pots, outhouses, well water (later, an indoor hydrant), sponge-bath wash pans, and stainless-steel No. 3 tubs. It was to be like this for the next 11 years.

I'm not sure whether to blame the lure of good Southern food, the culture shock, or both, but the weight issues began. There I was - the kid who was fat, nerdy, and talked "funny." The bullies among the black children in the immediate neighborhood and those on the school bus had a field day and ate away at my confidence and self-esteem. I was also targeted by some of my siblings, who were grappling with adolescence and battling demons having to do with the reasons my parents split. I used to joke that for a long time, I thought my name was Pig or the somewhat more creative Gut-Butt. As for talking "funny," I still mentally shake my head sometimes when people compliment me for having what they call a "commanding, arresting voice." When I was a child, that voice was ridiculed, "Oooo, why you talk so proper?" And I was repeatedly mocked. But that's Satan for you. He's a destiny killer and doesn't fight fair. At school, I socialized with some of the white children, that is, the ones who weren't also giving me flak for the aforementioned sins as well as for being black.

As loving a mother as she was, Mama, God bless her, wasn't perfect by a long shot. One of the areas in which I was a disappointment to her was that of my failure to stand up to the bullies. Sometimes I came home and told her about the verbal abuse I'd suffered. Mama would be frustrated that I'd let the bullies run over me, and I'd be scolded for cowardice. At times, she coached me on making snappy comebacks.

For the most part, I retreated into my daydreams and my books. Nowadays, children hear "put that phone down," or "put that computer game down." I often heard "put that book down" when I was summoned to do my neglected chores.

I also retreated into art. I was quite the child comic-strip creator. As I continued my creative-outlet pursuits, art gradually gave way to writing. Writing took me into another world, too. Writing was cathartic.

As a third-grader, I figured one of the best ways to test my writing talents and to earn some quick popularity would be to write a series of stories about a fictitious children's club whose members were my favorite classmates (usually, those I admired, envied, or had crushes on). The stories would be told through my eyes as a minor character. The club was first called *The Adventure Club*, then *The Supersonics*. I made up a wealthy sponsor, Michelle, who provided us with a clubhouse as we goofed off and solved a mystery or two. It was a cross between the club co-chartered by Trixie Belden (a fictitious teenage mystery solver featured in a series of books of which I was a fan at the time) and the gang from the Scooby-Doo cartoons. The stories indeed became quite popular with my peers. Even the teachers seemed to enjoy them. I wrote the stories through the rest of elementary school, all of junior high, and through my sophomore year of high school.

Five years after we came to Arkansas, my mother remarried. I was 11 years old, and the only child left living at home. We moved to my stepfather's small community of Woodson, Arkansas, where I went on to spend my adolescence and the first six years of adulthood. One thing I quickly found out was I didn't fit in with the children there, either.

Meanwhile, I excelled in school, and my budding writing efforts continued and expanded. In junior high, I became a member of the yearbook staff and continued to help produce yearbooks throughout high school. It was also in junior high that I put out a couple of corny, underground satirical newsletters and "renegade" stories that got me in mildly hot water. In high school, I joined the newspaper staff and started my first column, "Palmerphernalia," a take on my maiden name. That's when I began to realize that a career in newspaper journalism might be where I needed to direct my writing ability. That's also when my dream of being a columnist for a professional newspaper began.

I was making a name for myself in school, but a true social life evaded me. In high school, I was one of the celebrity smart kids and "publicly" popular. But the only social life I had was at school, in high school. I hung out with a small band of other misfits before classes began. Other than that, as a teenager in Woodson in the 1970s, I led a lonely, cloistered life. I had no car of my own and no permission to drive alone, even when I got a driver's license. Cell phones weren't even a twinkle in the eyes of Apple Inc. co-founder Steve Jobs. Landline phone calls from Little Rock to Wrightsville (a town only a few minutes drive away) were long distance and cost extra, let alone calls to Little Rock. Then, there were the summers that consisted of no summer job, no summer camp, no visits to the lake. I stayed cooped up in the house reading, watching TV, and helping with dinner while Mom was still at work. One summer, I was so bored I returned to my art roots, took what I learned in my junior-high art classes, and copied some of my classmates' portraits from the yearbook.

As a teen, I longed to have not only a boyfriend but the perfect one, a fellow like those I read about in those darned romance novels. High school yielded only a couple of short, awkward, embarrassing "relationships." Other encounters with the opposite sex hadn't been even that positive. I looked old for my age and attracted the attention of a few older men by whom I'm grateful not to have been physically victimized.

I was an honor student in school and received come-hithers from colleges all over the country as a finalist in the former National Achievement Scholarship Program. But I was a mama's girl, petrified at the thought of leaving home to go to school, and Mama was just as stressed at the thought. The summer before my senior year of high school, I attended a journalism workshop for "minority" students at the University of Arkansas in Little Rock. I took a liking to the journalism department chair at the time and knew that UALR (nowadays, branded as UA-Little Rock) was where I wanted to head to college.

After graduating 11th in my high school class, I went to UALR on a freshman scholarship that placed me in the University Scholars Program. Academically, that first year at UALR went great. I made the Dean's List and was inducted into a freshman honor society. Afterward, my route to my college degree became a whole lot more circuitous.

At the end of my freshman year, I was hired for my first newspaper job as city desk clerk at what was then one of two of Arkansas' statewide daily papers, the "Arkansas Democrat." At the same time, my eldest brother and then-sister-in-law gave me my first car, a green, 1973 Ford Maverick. Starting work at the newspaper in May of 1981, I spent two years as a clerk, four years as a consumer-affairs columnist, and two years as bridal editor before becoming a features writer and columnist. The "columnist" part came with my independent decision to continue a column begun by an editor who left the paper right after I wrote a guest column for her. My turn at the column had a rough beginning, but I gradually gained a following as I got my sea legs and started sharing personal experiences not just to share them, but to make some salient points based on what I was learning in that vast school we call life.

Meanwhile, my college career tanked in 1984. I didn't do so well combining school and work. It didn't help that gaining a job, and a car, had turned me on to the party life. Throw in a major romance that crashed and burned, add some burnout, and I had myself a perfect storm. My grades plummeted. So, the year I should have graduated, I began what I refer to as "a 14-year spring break." In 1998, nine years into my career as a features writer and columnist for what had become the "Arkansas Democrat-Gazette," I returned to UALR and in August 2000, finally earned a Bachelor of Arts degree in journalism.

Since 2006, I have also moonlighted as a freelance writer along with my husband, Renarda A. "Dre" Williams, a full-time freelance writer who founded The Umoja Network and "The Empowerment Initiative Online Newsletter." Later, I began my own arm of the company, "Make It Plain Ministries." I edit and ghostwrite Christian-testimony books for clients. The company is headed for growth as I look toward adding the role of writing coach to my repertoire.

I've gained a respectable reputation in the community, with the awards and honors to show for it. But it's been a tough road. As a child, I harbored some lofty expectations of adulthood. Carting around a bulky combination of low self-esteem and entitlement, I developed the idea that once I grew up, I'd automatically be handed recompense for all I'd suffered during my childhood.

Um, nope. My adulthood got off to a flying stop. I lived with my mother and stepfather for far too long after turning 18. The curfews continued, and with my newfound penchant for partying and the distances I had to drive to party, they became a big problem. As a college dropout still living with my parents, I gained a reputation with some family members as a slacker who'd "failed to launch." My problems with selfishness and lack of people skills didn't help. Worse, I eventually found myself without a car and was forced to go back to taking the Woodson Express bus to my job in downtown Little Rock. I was in a state of chronic anger and frustration until a visiting cousin saw my unhappiness and suggested I get an apartment. Realizing I couldn't fully live as an adult until I did so, I followed her suggestion.

But succeeding as an adult was still elusive. I especially felt like a failure in three areas in particular; areas I call *the three M's*:

- *Money*: I was not a good manager of it. (To this day, I struggle in this area.)
- *Men*: The Prince Charmings weren't piling up at my door, so I looked for love in all the wrong places and settled for relationships that, to put it very nicely, were a bad fit. I married at age 28, but the union lasted only seven years.
- *Mass*: My weight has fluctuated throughout the years, but I've spent only a very few years of my life smaller than "Queen Size." I constantly began fitness and/or healthy eating regimens but gave up sooner or later.

Then there were my spiritual shortcomings. I'd been in church all my life, mind you. I'd been baptized at age 11 and had volunteered (or was volunteered by my mother) for various roles and activities. But I didn't have a close relationship with God that would have helped me avoid a lot of mistakes and a world of pain. A friend of mine who went to be with the Lord some years ago once said that before she developed a close relationship with God, she saw Him as this "old white man in a long dress" who simply passed judgment on folks. The way my friend saw God is similar to how I saw Him for years. I thought He was a being who treated you well (sometimes) when you were good and would "get you" when you were bad.

For years, I walked around wrapped in a straitjacket of chronic, self-absorbed situational depression stemming from a reality that didn't jibe with my naive expectations. I assumed I just wasn't God's favorite. The things I'd hoped and prayed for the most seemed to always be out of reach. There would be nights I'd go to sleep, not wanting to wake up in the morning. Another wrong idea I had was that salvation was simply about avoiding Hell. I believed Christianity was a performance art and that salvation could be rescinded if I committed a sin and caught God on a bad day. A trap door would open up under me, just like in those old cartoons, and I'd go sliding down to Hell, where the devil would be waiting.

On the morning of March 14, 1997, I was told my mother had passed away in her sleep. My first thought was, "Who's going to pray for my sorry [self] now?" My mother had been my prayer warrior and, I felt, had been keeping me spiritually propped up all that time.

But my road to knowing God had already begun, via a TV preacher named Joyce Meyer.

Shortly after Mom passed, I was listening to Joyce on TV. She was preaching from Joshua 1, where God told Joshua, "Look, my servant Moses is dead. Now I need you to rise up and take my people into the promised land." Joyce told the viewing audience members that they might be in a Joshua position themselves. She gave the perfect for-instance: *If someone you depended on heavily for spiritual support has been moved on, via death or otherwise, and God is ready for you to stand on your own spiritual feet and possess the land, go on to the purpose He has for you.* I got goosebumps.

About four years later, I reconnected with a friend from the 1980s, a friend God had delivered from drug addiction. (I'd been too naïve to see her struggles.) She invited me to the weekly women's Bible Study classes at her church. It was in these classes that I began to realize who I was, and more important, whose I was. I learned that it was possible to be joyful in the Lord despite one's circumstances in the natural. I learned that I truly needed to first seek the kingdom of God, and His righteousness, and all my needs would be met (Matthew 6:33). I realized what Proverb 3:5-6 ("Trust in the Lord with all thine heart; and lean not unto thine own understanding. In all thy ways acknowledge him, and he shall direct thy paths.") really meant. Through this class, along with a couple of messages from the noted Bishop T.D. Jakes, I learned that marriage (at which I would soon have another chance) was a ministry, and I needed to concentrate on what I put into it rather than focus on what I got out of it. As a single woman, my job was to minister unto the Lord as if He were my spouse.

I had another important lesson to learn.

Growing up, I'd always felt like I was on the outside, looking in (I didn't even fit in with other nerds. At least, not with the ones who had superiority/snob complexes). As a high-school honors student and as an adult who'd made a name for herself as a newspaper columnist, I'd found myself in the peculiar position of being celebrated, but having few or no close friends. The close friendships I craved did not materialize at all, did not last long, or were simply less than fulfilling. As a young adult, I tried to fit in by joining organizations. I pledged a sorority in college but didn't find the sense of sisterhood I'd hoped for. Years later, I joined a prestigious group in the city and again found myself only with extra work to do. I was left feeling lonelier than ever and would end up exiting the groups I'd joined.

What I finally came to realize was I was not meant to get my identity from (or put all my efforts into) any group or clique. God had been gently but firmly setting me apart. He pointed out to me that I wasn't meant to fit in or be a member of the club. "I've called you to marketplace ministry," He revealed. "You are to move back and forth between groups, reflecting My love and My glory. If you join yourself with a particular group, you'll stay stuck in one place."

Look at the Apostle Paul. He talked of having to be all things to all people [1 Corinthians 9:19-23]. He was once a member of the Good Ol' Boys Club. He had it all but ultimately considered it dung compared to what he was doing for Christ [Phil. 3:4-8]. Also, because Paul was persecuted, he moved from place to place, preached Christ to the Gentiles, and spread the faith.

My main goal is to be more like Paul. And someday I'd like to be fully self-employed, especially as a speaker and coach traveling the world.

In the meantime, my job as a features writer, columnist, and society reporter-photographer is the main component of my marketplace ministry. When it comes to writing feature stories, I love highlighting positive things about my community. When it comes to writing "Let's Talk," my wit-and-wisdom column, I sometimes can literally feel the Holy Spirit taking control of my fingers and guiding me into tapping out works with a perspective that flesh and blood didn't reveal to me. Now, the devil has no problem trying to make me feel like a failure as a writer. But any time I start to feel that way, some readers will come along and tell me how much they enjoy my writing and how much a positive difference I made in their lives. I know that's a hug from God.

As for those three M's I struggled with:

Men: I'm happily remarried.

Mass: I hit the gym five days a week and began eating a plant-based diet, determined to make middle age look AND feel good.

Money: I still have problems with managing it and with not making enough of it. But I remind myself that God is my source. And as I continue to delight myself in/trust in the Lord, I look forward to seeing what He has ahead.

Meanwhile, I enjoy lifting as I climb, giving a few words of encouragement here and there to the girls and young women who are coming behind me. I like to think I'm not only encouraging them to reach their destinies, but also helping them to come to the full realization of who they are faster than I did.

Dear hearts, please allow me to offer you some advice based on my life experiences, including past mistakes:

- **Know that you are special**, and you are valuable, no matter how much anybody tries to convince you otherwise. There are no throwaway people on this earth. And there's no need to try to be anyone else. The Creator made you just the way He intended to make you. Bask in that.

- **It's not cliché:** Yes, girls/women can do anything. It seems ridiculous to have to say that in 2020, but you can do anything, despite any lingering, persistent sexism or any discouraging headlines about there being so few women occupying the corner office at the biggest corporations. Do you have a desire, a dream, or a gift that would take you into a realm in which few women move? Push past any fear of failure (or of being given a hard time by the fellows who dominate the field). Getting to where you want to go might not be a cakewalk, but if you're meant to be there, you are meant to overcome any obstacles that present themselves.

- **Speaking of obstacles,** know that the devil is not your friend. He will use people to try to tear you down, telling you you're not pretty enough, thin enough, smart enough, or cool enough. You may not "fit in" anywhere. You may be made to feel rejected. Consider the possibility that the area of your life in which the most attacks come is the very area where your strongest giftings and callings lie. This could be the very area in which God plans to use you to make a powerful, devil-defeating impact in this world.

- **Do not lose sight of your God-given vision.** The devil is also a master of sending not only weapons of mass destruction but weapons of mass distraction to separate people from their destiny. Don't let something that's not healthy or beneficial to you interrupt, delay, or impede you in becoming all you were meant to be. (Yes, I especially mean the "cool" friends who want to pull you down to their partying, substance-abusing level or that romantic partner who may put you in a situation you can't easily walk away from.) Set your goals and be like that horse whose owner has placed blinders around its eyes to keep the horse from seeing behind or beside it (and therefore becoming distracted) as it performs a task. You may have to go through some lonely times. You can make those times work to your benefit. You are on your way to greatness. Prepare.

- **Be on the lookout for ways to serve others**, but don't lose sight of taking care of YOU. Ever been on a plane and heard the flight attendant, while giving safety instructions, tell parents to put THEIR masks on first and put their young children's masks on second, if the cabin should suffer a sudden drop in pressure? In order to be a blessing to others, you have to make sure you are in a position (spiritually, mentally, physically, etc.) to be that blessing. Do not get caught up in people-pleasing, especially to the point where you are not taking time to hang out with God via prayer and study. Exercise your body, eat healthy, and enjoy your favorite recreational activities. It's all about self-love. It is not vanity or narcissism to take care of your "temple" (body) and its "bell tower" (your mind) so that you CAN step up and run the world!

- **Take advantage of living** in what is now considered a global society. One of the advantages of working as a newspaper features writer is that even more than those books I read as a child, my job introduced me to people and cultures I might not have come into contact with otherwise. This further educated me and broadened my horizons as well as showed me the disadvantage of "fitting in" with one group and, possibly, failing to venture outside that group! I am on friendly terms with members of Little Rock's Filipino, Asian, Indian, and Latino communities, as well as people from African and Caribbean countries. In today's society, social media, technology, (relatively) affordable travel, and corporate diversity programs have given us easier ways to get to know those who don't look or act like us. Get to know them. Celebrate them. Be enriched by them as you enrich them.

- **Life is a journey**. Don't be so caught up in getting to the destination that you fail to enjoy the journey. Every moment is precious. Stop and smell those roses. Celebrate your victories, but don't despise your failures. These are valuable lessons that pave the way to your success.

Having been the answer to my mother's prayer, I have this as my ultimate goal: to be a vehicle by which the prayers of others are answered.

May this be your goal too.

Girl Power

Phyllis Marie Marshall-Hodges (Born April 4, 1958)

Author, Fitness Specialist and Consultant, Entrepreneur

Bestselling author of 8 Years of Unforgettable History

Term: Current

Previous Title(s) Held: Clergy and Television Personality

Phyllis Hodges CFT., LHM is a bestselling author of three books. In addition to being a fitness guru, she is also a wife, mother, and grandmother. Married to her high school sweetheart for 46 years, she resides in Little Rock, Arkansas.

Introducing Dr. Marion Williams ...

During my research for this book, I found out about a female doctor from Arkansas, who is a psychiatrist.

Dr. Marion Williams is an incredible woman. How courageous for an African American woman to enroll in medical school at the age of 40!

I was introduced to her by her brother, a former church member of mine. He brought her to my Wellness Center for a massage. I had no idea who she was, but was blessed when I put 'two and two together' and realized this was the same lady who had come to me for a massage 'back in the day.'

The key to this story is every woman, no matter the age or background needs to invest in yourself for the **HEALTH** of it!

Enjoy her story!

Multiple Gracious Opportunities

Dr. Marion Williams

The truth is anything that can be thought of as an accomplishment; in my opinion, it is a combination of multiple gracious opportunities.

My journey began in 1946 when a beautiful, brilliant, and gentle warrior gave me passage into this life. My soul can vividly remember a time before my language that I was surrounded by her. Her voice made sounds that were the epitome of what "soothing" really was, and she became the conductor who led me to so many wonderful ambassadors.

Mama ushered me through elementary and high school as a masterful conductor. The name of my elementary school was *Log Bayou*, where there were two classes per room until the 7th and 8th grades. My high school, *Wolfe Project High School*, was a long bus ride from my house. In those two academic institutions, I met many ambassadors: Mrs. Green, Mrs. Smith, Mr. Powell, Mrs. McGowan, Mr. and Mrs. Richard Smith, Mrs. Wimberly, Mr. Lowe, Mrs. Pearl Shouse, and Professor Thompson who was a very gifted community musician. These ambassadors taught beyond the outdated and discarded textbooks and soared miles beyond any routine teaching plans. They taught humanities and modern (really modern) history. They inspired me to start dreaming of college and beyond. I was introduced to Bach, Chopin, and other great masters. I also learned to focus in a different and beautiful way.

Lonnie Thompson, my grandfather, was another skillful conductor who was born on Feb. 3, 1896. He was a brilliant man with a 3rd-grade education. He offered me an agenda in which all people were judged by their actions and could become whatever they dreamed. He firmly believed, in 1954, women should be educated and trained in the areas of their interests and talents.

"If you want to," Grandfather said with vigor, "you can become a welder, or a banker, or a doctor, or a farmer, or anything baby girl."

Not only did he say those words, he freely gave his support and blessings.

My disliking of hoeing cotton quickly ruled out the farming career. With the guidance of the great conductors in my life, I wanted to go to college to do something in science. The opportunity to attend college required hard work by my family on the farm, domestic work for hire, scholarships, work-study programs, and loans. Often money came from home. As it turns out, all who were surrounded by my mother became Conductors in training. One of my fondest memories was getting $3.47 from my little brother during my freshman year in college.

A college education was a source of community pride, and the "village" was indeed supportive in many ways. With each trip home, there were bits of cash, wonderful sendoffs, cakes, cookies, and gourmet meals, prepared by surrogates (mamas, aunts, uncles, and church members). Instinctively, everyone seemed to know that a village was always required for any measure of improvement.

At the ripe old age of 17, my college experience was filled with a social life and events such that my world had never-before-seen. Games, social events, sports, dates, and love existed everywhere. My focus of learning and staying the academic path that my high school days and my God-given conductors prepared me for was taking somewhat of a backseat in "my new world." This new world of mine was sometimes interrupted with academics, but during those interruptions, there were giants who led me to seek academic pursuits, a measure of desiring knowledge, and somewhat of a will to achieve a career.

I had some wonderful opportunities during my college years, and one of those opportunities was a student job at a prestigious national laboratory in the Midwest. What a source of pride and joy that was for me! I was introduced to the fascinating real-world of industrial chemistry. What an honor! During my summer tenure there, I realized that I was ill-prepared to participate in the real world of science.

An employee of the Institute told me very loudly in a public forum, "Your best bet is to return to the community of *your kind* and start a protest march against inadequacies of any sort."

I took that as a hurtful and personal slap. I initially responded by shedding bitter tears, and for a moment, instead of feeling pride that I was selected for such a prestigious summer job, I felt shame and a sense of undeserving. With the nurturing support of my conductor, I changed my mind. I began to reexamine the routes to my goal. I was beginning to realize that my "new world" had interrupted my academics, not the other way around, and I had missed a few key elements. So, I came back to my community not to start a protest march as suggested earlier, but to review, revisit, and retake some of the science courses that had taken me earlier. The effort was made with hopes of improving my background in some of the basic courses. I enrolled in a local community college which had an excellent reputation in the sciences. The college allowed me to enroll but warned me that I was ill-prepared for the course. I was given a very safe but sterile environment. During the initial part of the course, I was managing a good passing score but was given the option of dropping the course. As the course grew more difficult, my grade suffered, but dropping the course was no longer an option, and I learned much more than my grade reflected. Both the teacher and I gained a great deal of respect for each other, which was an unexpected gift. I was very, very sad about the outcome of the course. I considered quitting but changed my mind. With the nurturing and support of my conductors, I renewed my energy towards strengthening my background and moving forward. Moving forward became more of a challenge than I expected as I was faced with trying to learn new material while I was completing the learning of the old material. This period of time was complicated by a brand-new marriage and a baby on the way. I managed to get my college degree the year that sweet baby was born. Suddenly, there were more and more things that I did not know, and by now, the demands had grown. I was rudely introduced to the world of multitasking. It felt as if my efforts were going exponentially backward, and when I considered forging ahead to find my career, I thought it was too hard to go on. But I changed my mind. With the nurturing and support of my conductors, I was ready to start learning the arts (there are many) of multi-tasking.

At this point in my pursuit, I was blessed with a beautiful baby girl. Her mere existence taught me so much about being a mother. From her beginning, she cherished love and exhibited marvelous work ethics, and even as a little one, she joined as a supporter of my quest to find a career.

I found a way to enroll in a Master of Science program and a Medical Technology program. I completed both simultaneously, and along the way I encountered Dr. Lothar Schafer, an ambassador who is a brilliant scientist. He breathed encouragement into my very soul, and I became more and more interested in learning. As I pulled further and further away from self-doubt, I really began to believe there was a career for me. As it turned out, all who

Girl Power: Dr. Marion Williams

surrounded Mama were in training to become conductors, so my brother shuttled me from location to location using his time, energy, and money.

Following the Master of Science program and the Medical Technology program, I went to work in a hospital laboratory and eventually a local paper mill that afforded me a salary, benefits, and the opportunity to live very near to my conductors. What joy! But I still had a yearning that I had not yet found my career.

My wonderful grandfather finished his work as a conductor for me on this earth a few days before his 80th birthday. He left lovely memories and patterns for me to follow, but my heart was heavy for a long time. My beautiful mother mourned and grieved his death for many years that followed, but she eventually got into a different rhythm of living and refined her capacity to be a conductor for me, all while she was promoting the strength and character of the community. She had the art of multi-tasking down packed.

Restlessness began to search for me with the haunting thought that my career had not yet caught up with me. Didn't my grandfather say, many years ago, that I could be anything I wanted to be? Even a doctor? Yes, but that was before I was approaching middle age, wasn't it? I was already much too old to consider medical school, and I thought, "I mustn't waste my time thinking about it," but I changed my mind.

My lone ambassador (Mama) always had my best interest in her heart and mind. She preached that it was not practical for me to go for such a pursuit, and she thought that my dream was worse than a bad idea. I had never been in a world without my mother's full-fledged support, but I knew age would come my way no matter what was going on. I could not bear the thought of looking back and wondering what could have been, so I began the pursuit without my mother's routine conductor role in my life. This was, however, a temporary injunction and my brother, sister-in-law, nieces, nephews, and friends came forth with loads of support and a great deal of encouragement. One such friend was the kind and brilliant Mr. Wendell Hunt, whom I met as a teenager, and in Sept of 2019, he left this world a much better place. After many attempts to get into medical school, with God's grace, I finally got an acceptance letter, and after a circuitous route, I gained access and became a freshman medical student at the age of 40.

Prior to starting medical school, I petitioned the Almighty to provide me with teachers who had an interest in wanting to teach me medicine. My prayers were answered, and I met more ambassadors than I could begin to name who poured knowledge and encouragement into my being. To name a few: Mrs. Patricia Johnson remains one of my prayer partners to this day, Dr. Phil Rayford continued to push me even in dark times and convinced me that knowledge builds on knowledge, Dr. Richard Wheeler never gave up on me and never allowed me to give up on myself, and Dr. Gilmore believed in me and taught me to believe in the skills that I had and more importantly in the skills that I would acquire. An entire book can be written detailing the beauty of the training that goes into training physicians.

I graduated from medical school in May 1990, and my mother was on hand to celebrate with me. She had originally believed medical school was a bad idea, but she changed her mind and resumed her role as my conductor. She gave up 37 years of her personal history and moved with me to West Virginia while I did my residency training. She also provided primary care for a young daughter who was born during medical school and a son who was born during her residency. I felt well trained, and I was treated with care, concern, and respect throughout my residency training. That training program was filled with beautiful ambassadors.

I have been privileged to work in West Virginia, Odessa, Texas, Malvern, and Little Rock, Arkansas, and Lubbock, TX. Those practices have brought me joy and the assurance that I have chosen my career wisely. During my work in Odessa, I met a musical genius, Mr. Bennet, who took me on as a piano student after approximately a 32-year hiatus. That training now allows me to enjoy restoring my soul with beloved hymns under the direction of his esteemed and beautiful colleague, Mrs. Joy Moutos, in Lubbock, Texas.

My mother resigned her earthly role as my conductor in November of 2013. I was sure that I would die of pure grief. As it turns out, all who were surrounded by my mother were in training to be conductors. A man of God, my brother, stood "in the gap and petitioned the Almighty to manage my grief."

My heart continues to ache because I miss her so deeply, but I carry so many wonderful memories of the time that I was blessed to be on this earth while she existed. I am happy for my journey, and I relish the routes and the grace that has led me to this point.

I have tried to be clear that anything resembling success on my part is really a journey with conductors who have accompanied me on life's journey, with stops all along the way, to meet wonderful ambassadors.

Kim Yarbrough (Born December 18, 1977)

Illustrator

Girl Power Illustrator

Term: 2019

Additional Title(s) Held: Nail Technician and Registered Dental Assistant

---

Kim Yarbrough is an author and illustrator. Her book, "Frannie And The Big Birthday Wish," was written and illustrated by the talented author. She also served as illustrator for the book, "Queenie."

Kim is a member of the Junior League of Little Rock and mother of eight.

Girl Power

Introducing Kim Yarbrough ...

This is a delightful story to share.

I was scrolling the internet and ran across some beautiful drawings and illustrations of ethnic children. Then, I saw a creative book about a family of color. The cover caught my attention because as an author

I wanted to meet this local artist/author. I reached out to her, and a meeting was scheduled. During the meeting, it was as though I was listening to myself on a recorder. We had so much in common.

I shared my story, my vision, and my upcoming project with her. At that time, Kim and I decided to collaborate on our work.

The rest, as they say, is **HISTORY**!

A Borrowed Girl with No Identity, an "In-between"

Kim Yarbrough

"Worse than being black is being 'mixed.' Children who are part of both races 'don't belong anywhere.' Colored folks won't have 'em because they're half white; white folks won't have 'em 'cause they're colored, so they're just in-betweens, don't belong anywhere." **Harper Lee, To Kill A Mockingbird**

I was in second grade. I remember looking out the window of the shuttle bus as I was en route to the military base where my dad was stationed. It was snowing heavily, and I was slowly writing my name on the glass window with my finger. For whatever reason, my mother began to give me the "you are special" adoption speech. Up to this point, I had assumed that I was blonde and blue-eyed (not in the literal sense) because I did not see in color, at least not yet. I did not see myself any different from my younger brother.

Whether I realized I was different or not, others had undeniably known that I "did not fit" because I looked different. I was a mixed-race child amongst a primarily Caucasian environment. To make matters worse, I was mixed-race when it was considered taboo. Therefore, little was discussed regarding interracial relationships and children.

The only thing that was common about "mix-breeds" was that it was frowned upon. Learning that I was adopted revealed to me why everyone always stared or asked my mother if my brother and I were both her kids.

In third grade, I began to encounter unusual obstacles in Ms. Petre's class. Ms. Petre believed "mixed children had learning and behavior problems." She sat back and watched one morning as my classmates moved their desks away from me and stretched their eyes out to look more Asian. They begged me not to throw bombs at them and said my nose was big. Crying out for help, I was told to suck it up and stop acting like a spoiled brat.

No matter what I did, Ms. Petre did not trust me. She would criticize my handwriting and reading. As things escalated, she would isolate me from my peers by making me sit alone, tying me to my seat, or even locking me in her small broom closet. Day after day, she would randomly accuse me of rolling my eyes or mumbling, which served as a cue for the class to bully me, both verbally and physically. One morning she began yelling at me. For whatever reason, I decided to stand up for myself by talking back. All I remember was seeing a flash of light and simultaneously feeling pain as I saw the warm blood dripping from my arm.

I sat in the school office with a paper towel as my mother and Ms. Petre both agreed that my behavior was manipulative and brought violent reactions out of others. (Apparently, this was why Ms. Petre had been compelled to throw a textbook at me.) The outcome of my assault ended with my desk being moved to the back of the classroom.

Ms. Petre insisted I was academically challenged and assigned me *special* homework. She and I continued to clash, so much so, that I was assigned to a school counselor.

My counselor was the absolute opposite of Ms. Petre. She was kind, and she had long, red, curly hair. I looked forward to seeing her twice a week. She made me feel special and safe. One day she told me that she believed I was smart. She wanted me to take some tests, and I eagerly cooperated. I will never forget Ms. Petre's face when my counselor and principal confronted her on her reasoning for putting me in her developmental reading group. Thankfully for me, three days a week, my counselor picked me up and walked me upstairs to the fourth-grade class for reading. This was something I looked forward to because I now had a new teacher who gave me nothing but praises. She was an ally.

Ms. Petre's consistent complaints of being uncomfortable around me finally resulted in me being transferred to another classroom. The day I was transferred to Mrs. Barnett's class, I was greeted with, "I know all about you, Kim, and I have my eye on you, little girl."

No one else stood up for me. I felt as though I deserved to be mistreated. As a child, I felt that I was no more than a puppy that was selected out of a pet store. No matter the situation, people's manners seemed non-existent as they could never fight the urge to ask my parents, "Is she yours? What is she?"

"Oh, this is our daughter," my parents would reply. "She's mixed. We adopted her."

During these conversations, I felt the only missing elements were a red carpet and someone to present my mother with her Nobel Peace Prize for adopting her *refugee*, *mixed*, *orphaned* daughter. I was never a refugee or an orphan, but that is how I felt. I was a borrowed child, their stand-in. Being multi-racial didn't help make things easier. My Caucasian parents could not relate to the social torment I experienced being called things like *mixed breed*, *twinkie*, *oreo*, or *Heinz 57*.

"What would Jesus do?" My mom's reasoned. This did very little to settle my issues. Out of all the hurtful scenarios I encountered growing up, the one that stands out the most surrounds my grandfather. There is no doubt in my mind the love he had for me. He called me his little *black-eyed pea*, but his statement that evening would only serve to confirm that I was someone's mistake. It was dinner, and I was sitting right next to him.

"I feel discrimination in town," I began. "People cut in front of me in line, called me a chink, or a n____ gook."

"Kim, you keep a chip on your shoulder," my mother insisted. "You see prejudice everywhere."

"I have dark hair too," my grandfather said as he slammed his fist down in anger. "You look white enough to marry a white man! End of discussion."

My grandfather, who had never apologized to a soul, later apologized to me. Although forgiveness was easy, the hurt left a life-long scar etched in my heart.

It made me hate how I looked. I felt like trash and that I was a nobody.

If I were lucky, maybe I could marry a white man. Was that all I was? Was that all I could look forward to?

Part of me diminished. All I ever was, was a title. I accepted that I was nothing but an adopted girl. A borrowed girl. A mixed-race, slow learning girl. A discarded girl. An ugly girl. A fat girl. A stupid girl. I was a girl that required an adjective, an explanation, or an introduction, to justify my existence, my presence, or my inclusion. I could not just be Kim. I didn't even know who "Kim" was.

As a young adult, I connected my emotional scars with my adoption. You can sugarcoat adoption all you want, but the truth be told, there are psychological traumas that go unaddressed. I was devastated because I knew that I had been robbed of my heritage. I was a person with no people. I didn't have any cultural roots.

Growing up, I envied my brother and friends, not because they were athletic or had great toys but because they could look into their mothers' eyes and see themselves. I wanted to see the physical resemblance of me, in my mother, and to know that I came from her blood. I wanted to know that she loved me unconditionally and not because she felt sorry for me. No matter how many self-help books I read, there was an unfilled void that lay heavily upon my chest. It was like an unexplainable pain or an unquenchable thirst. It left me feeling like an un-squeezed sponge, leaking with sorrows and lies.

How could a mother, no matter her situation, give her child away?

There had to be something wrong with me, I deduced. I was 25 years old when I came across an excerpt from the book "To Kill A Mockingbird" by author Harper Lee that I identified with.

> *"Worse than being black is being 'mixed.' Children who are part of both races don't belong anywhere. Colored folks won't have 'em because they're half white; white folks won't have 'em 'cause they're colored, so they're just in-betweens, don't belong anywhere."* I was an "in-between."

I remember waking one morning and deciding that I would find my biological mother. For years, my attempts to track her were unsuccessful, but not this time. By the next afternoon, I had tracked her down by piecing together her past online. She was the owner of a nail salon in Alaska. I went there to see her, but she'd just flown to Seattle to be with family. After several hours of trying to understand broken English, I was able to convince the women at the salon that I was her "long lost daughter." Hours later, I was on the phone with my biological mother! The conversation revealed that I had four brothers (one of which was lost in Vietnam.). The other three were artists like me, with December birthdays, just like me. Within a few days, I would come face-to-face with the woman who carried me in her womb. It would be the first time in my life to look into a woman's face, to see myself in the reflection of her eyes, and to know that is of where I came. I would no longer be a person with no people and no longer a person without cultural roots, or so I thought.

Within hours of meeting me, my biological mother left in the night. A week later, she sent a text message explaining that I was not who she had envisioned and meeting me was just too overwhelming. She strongly encouraged me to lose weight and stated that the nail industry would never take me seriously because my obesity made me appear slothful and lazy.

Having a relationship with her was not to be. I was too late.

I cried so terribly that I expected to die from my pain. I did not expect to wake up. Had it not been solely for my children, I did not want to wake up. A childhood dream and hope had been abruptly diminished in only a matter of days. Words cannot describe how unworthy of a human being I felt. To have a mother deny you not once, but twice? Adjectives could not serve my pain the justice owed. I could not help but focus on how she and my biological father, although divorced, would have more children and keep them. I was their mistake.

So now what?

It was already difficult to reconcile as a child things people say like, "You are special" or "You are a blessing" when you know that your parents didn't want you as a baby.

Who doesn't love babies?

That painful experience with my biological mother caused a realization within me. I had never *lost* my identity. I had never *had* an identity, and as sad as it sounds, it isn't an uncommon practice amongst girls or even women.

Think about it. Despite a great deal of progress in the past half-century, gender-specific stereotypes persist. People continue to associate qualities like strength, intellect, and autonomy with masculinity, while they associate qualities like weakness, emotion, and dependence with femininity. Women may consciously reject these stereotypes and find that stereotypes still affect their sense of identity.

From the day you were born, your parents dressed you in ruffles and pastels, spoiled you with baby dolls and sent you to sleep with fairytales of princesses and true love. How many of you are told, "You are so pretty!" Why, pretty? Why not, "You are so smart!"? In school, you are or were encouraged to participate in gender accepted sports and exposed to careers that are better suited for women. This is all well and good, except, what if you were the girl who did not want to be like everyone else? You weren't a misfit, but you went against the norms.

As women, we are encouraged to be strong, but within boundaries. Many of us go from one title to another - from daughter to wife, to mother, but who are we really? Each title comes with a set of responsibilities. I love my children with every microscopic cell in my body. Like *most* mothers, there is not one possession, aspiration, or desire that I would spare sacrificing for the betterment of my children, but if you do not take the time to nurture yourself, you can easily become lost within your title and rob yourself of being the best version of you.

As an adoptee, everything I ever encountered that was negative, I blamed on not knowing my biological mother. Because that natural tie was severed, I felt that I was, in turn, broken. I remember watching reunion stories on television and envisioning how my own would be. I expected that a reunion would heal me and provide me with something I could not cultivate myself. I was mistaken.

Being the best version of you begins with identifying what inspires you.

What is it that fuels your heart and motivates you to be better than the day before?

Not what you are expected to do, but the instinct that drives you naturally to be unique and unafraid. I immediately began evaluating who I was. I came to the self-realization that you can know exactly where you come from, trace your entire genealogy records, and still not "know who you are." Being reunited with the past was never my key to my future me. I had to learn to love Kim.

But how? How do I love myself?

Loving everyone else in my life came easy because that is how I was trained. My first step was acknowledging that I was not a "bad kid" and that children only behave as well as they are treated. This next realization triggered a newfound mindset for me altogether. Secondly, I would no longer associate with negative people. I began to operate my mind like a business, meaning that every encounter was rendered a "business" transaction, and I would not deplete my energy levels by giving two positives for someone's negative. From there, I reclaimed my power! I would no longer give my power away! No one has the power to affect my day, my career, my future, or my life! Yes, I felt rejected by my mother. Yes, I felt pain from outside sources. I had to tell myself, "Move away from the fire, Kim!" Soon, I was no longer interested in the "tea" at work because I had begun a self-realization journey, and wisdom "brews" knowledge. My friends and family instantly recognized a change in me. Many were excited for me, and others became distant. I called that the "weeding" process. I was repositioning my "team" with God as my Captain, and the devil was intimidated.

Finally, I saw myself as a WHOLE person. I was no longer an "in-between." I was an "everything!" No longer would I wait for someone to love me. I would love me! No longer would I wait for someone to repair me because I was never broken. In fact, I was resilient.

I won't lie to you. I still experience sadness and occasional bouts of pain. The difference now is that I acknowledge the sadness instead of suppressing it. I re-channel the pain and reabsorb the energy as fuel to feed the hunger inside of me.

The words my biological mother spoke did not seal my fate. They, in fact, inspired my future. I had been in the nail industry for over 20 years when I met her. Within a year of our encounter, I would not only be the first of 15 women selected internationally between Canada and the United States, but I would be published and recognized worldwide by the most renowned and trusted nail industry source, *NAILS Magazine*.

As a young girl or woman reading this book today, walk away knowing that it doesn't matter your genealogy, your physical attributes, environment, nor your circumstances. You were born more than powerful enough to fulfill every title that you take on successfully.

Regardless of nature, choice, or accident, **YOU** alone have the amazing ability to adapt and adequately feed your personal endeavors, as long as you remember to **CELEBRATE** the **WOMAN** in you!

Final Thoughts

Girl Power, That's You!

Girls (mothers, daughters, wives) use your power, voice, strength, mind, and most importantly – use your faith. While looking beautiful, be bold. Consider yourself the boss, leading lady, and queen of cuisine.

How do you see yourself?

Represent, it matters. Do what you love. Be true to yourself. Your passion is so important. Feel the power. You have it. Now it is time to use it. Be what you desire. This is your life. Live it to the fullest. Remember, you only have one life to live, so make it worth your while. Many people are cheering you on. You can do it. You deserve this. Many will follow. You are the female role model the world has been waiting on.

It doesn't matter your skin tone, your culture, your religion, or your economic background - you're the one that we've been waiting on. Feel included, safe, and equipped. Go for it! You are educated, well equipped, prepared, and incredibly wise. Use your strength. Be fit in various areas, including physically, emotionally, spiritually, and financially. *Girl Power*, that's you!

How can we make a difference for other females?

I think back over my life and realize that my mom is the leading lady who is my hero. At an early age she told me, "Nothing is impossible if you only believe." Mom is a strong lady who believed that a *real* mother should take care of her children. She didn't do a lot of talking but instead demonstrated an awesome strong life for us. Mom didn't work outside the home until my siblings and I were enrolled in school. She was a true homemaker and ran a tight ship preparing healthy meals and assigning chores. Mom realized that one day we would be grown and gone and was determined to be the first teacher that we ever had.

During the designing phase for the cover of *Girl Power*, I reflected upon women whom most people view as powerful female role models. I quickly decided to add a mirror to the back cover. I wanted those who admired the book's beauty, and the stunning women depicted to also see themselves as God made them: beautifully and wonderfully made.

Whether it's Oprah, Michelle Obama, Beyoncé, Megan Markle, Ellen DeGeneres, or even my mom or me, I want you to remember that while we may be different, we all have something in common. That's the great thing about being one of God's creations. We all are special and different. God didn't make any copies. This is even true for twins; they are different also. They may have the same physical attributes, but their fingerprints are different.

Let me share with you our similarities. We all are females. When we are cut, we all bleed the same red blood! When God created us, He gave all of us the same measure of faith. It's left up to us individually if we want to build up our faith or not. There's something else we share: We can be sure that if we are born, we will all die one day. ("A time to be born and a time to die." **Ecclesiastes 3:2 NIV**)

So, it's time to live our best lives. This *Girl Power* book is full of examples of incredible life stories of women who beat the odds. They all exemplify *Girl Power*. We all have a story to tell, and each of our stories matter.

Girl Power - it is!

Phyllis Hodges CFT., LHM

About the Author

Bestselling Author, Phyllis Hodges' first manuscript was a self-motivational book entitled, "A Divine Connection." Her sophomore title, "8 Years of Unforgettable History," is an international living history book that can be found around the globe, in schools, libraries, bookstores, and many homes. The author is in the process of completing three more books.

As a member of the clergy, she teaches the Word of God with an emphasis on health and healing. She studied in the theology program at Missionary Baptist Seminary and Agape College and Full Counsel School of Ministry. She's a television personality who produced and hosted the first television talk show in the '80s. The "30 Plus" talk show aired on ABC, Channel 7 courtesy of an African American female. Now, she makes public appearances on various television shows as a "fitness expert."

As a fitness specialist, Phyllis owned the first and only faith-based fitness and wellness center in North Little Rock, Arkansas, from 2000-2019. The *Carousel Fit-4-Life Wellness Center* was previously located in the historic district of North Little Rock, Arkansas, in the downtown *Argenta District*.

Phyllis currently serves as a consultant and fitness specialist at numerous fitness centers and nursing homes. Her diverse fitness certifications were obtained globally through various health and fitness institutions such as the American Council on Exercise (ACE), International Sports Science Association (ISSA), and The Arthritis Foundation Institute.

Phyllis is affiliated with numerous nonprofit organizations and serves on local and international boards. As an athlete, she has run marathons for over eleven years.

Married to her first love, Byron Hodges, whom she met in high school, the two have two adult children and three young adult grandchildren.

To contact the author:

Email: carouselfit4life@gmail.com

Website: doyouphylme.com

Facebook: @GIRL Power

Instagram: @GIRL Power

YouTube: Phyllis Hodges

More Girl Power

Girl Power: Fun Facts

Arkansas Female Celebrities & Noteworthy Personalities

(Presented in alphabetical order)

Dr. Maya Angelou (Poet)
Born April 4, 1928 (Died May 28, 2014) – St. Louis Mo, Raised in Stamps, AR

Chelsie Clinton (Journalist)
Born February 27, 1980 – Little Rock, AR

Hillary Rodham Clinton (Former First Lady of the US & Secretary of State)
Born October 26, 1947 – Chicago, IL

Florence Beatrice Price (Musical Composer, Pianist, Organist, Music Teacher)
Born April 9, 1887 (died June 3, 1953) - Little Rock, AR

Mary Steenburgen (Actress)
Born February 8, 1953 - Newport, AR

Phyllis Yvonne Stickney (Actress and Comedian)
Little Rock, AR

Cheryl Underwood (Comedian & Television Personality)
Born October 28, 1963 – Little Rock, AR

Alice Louise Walton (Walmart Heiress)
Born October 7, 1949 - Newport, AR

**Special note: Although not relative to Arkansas, it is noteworthy that in 2019 the Miss America, Miss Teen USA, Miss USA, and Miss Universe we simultaneously held by African American women.

Cover Ladies

The ladies on the cover of this book have all played a significant role in depicting the power and influence of females.

Oprah Gail Winfrey – born, January 29, 1954

Oprah Winfrey is an American media executive, actress, talk show host, television producer, and billionaire philanthropist. Her alma mater is Tennessee State University. She was born in Kosciusko, Mississippi.

Dr. Michelle LaVaugh Robinson Obama – born, January 17, 1964

Michelle Obama, born in Chicago, Illinois, is an American lawyer and author. She was the first African American First Lady of the United States (2009-2017). Married to the 44th President of the United States (Barack Obama), Michelle is the mother of two daughters and known as the Mom-in-Chief. She was educated at Princeton University (1981-1985) and Harvard University (1985-1988).

Beyonce Giselle Knowles-Carter – born, September 4, 1981

Beyonce is an American singer, songwriter, record producer, dancer, and actress. Born and raised in Houston, Texas, Beyonce performed in various singing and dancing competitions as a child. She is married to Jay-Z (American Rapper) and the mother of three. She was educated at *Kinder High School For The Performing and Visual Arts School* in Houston, Texas.

Girl Power: Fun Facts

Ellen DeGeneres – born, January 26, 1965

Ellen Lee DeGeneres is a well-known American comedian, television host, actress, writer, and producer. She starred in the sitcom, *Ellen*, from 1994-1998 and hosted her syndicated TV talk show, *The Ellen DeGeneres Show*. She is also an advocate for LGBTQ rights. Educated at Grace King High School, Atlanta High School, and the University of New Orleans, Ellen majored in communication and left after one semester. She was born in Metairie, LA.

Rachel Meghan Markle – born, August 4, 1981

American born, Meghan Markle, Duchess of Sussex, is a former actress and current member of the British Royal Family. Meghan was born in Canoga Park, Los Angeles, California. During her studies at Northwestern University, she began playing small roles in television series and films. She is married to Prince Harry and the mother of one son, Archie Harrison Mountbatten-Windsor.

Rose Marie Bolden-Wright – born, February 24, 1938

Rose Wright (aka Mama Rose) is the mother of "Girl Power" author, Phyllis Hodges. Mrs. Wright has five adult children whom she adores. She has seven grandchildren and eleven great-grandchildren.

After retiring as a former nutritionist for various Little Rock schools, Mama Rose opened a childcare and a boutique business, "Mama Rose Corner."

Mama Rose was born in Little Rock, Arkansas, and educated at the historic Dunbar High School and the University of Arkansas Fayetteville.

Phyllis Marie Marshall-Hodges CFT., LHM, born April 4, 1958

Phyllis Hodges is the bestselling author of the living history book, "8 Years of Unforgettable History." She also wrote and self-published "A Divine Connection," which is a self-help testimonial and fitness book. Phyllis' story, "School Days," was included in the compilation "Writing Our Lives Volume II, A Southern Storytellers Anthology" and her story "A Reflection of My Living History" was included in "Writing Our Lives Volume III, A Southern Storytellers Anthology." The author is currently working on three additional books.

In addition to writing books, Phyllis is an entrepreneur, fitness specialist and consultant, clergy, and television personality. During her time on television, she interviewed many greats such as Muhammad Ali, Sinbad, The Whispers, just to name a few.

She received theology education at Missionary Baptist Seminary and Agape College and has received a numerous amount of global health and fitness certificates from across the globe including ACE American Council on Exercise, ISSA International Sports Science Association, and the Arthritis Institute.

Born in Little Rock, Arkansas, Phyllis has been married to her high school sweetheart for 46 years. The two have two adult children and three young adult grandchildren.

Girl Power: Fun Facts

History Makers & Trailblazers

16 African American Women that have served for the Arkansas House of Representatives (presented in alphabetical order)

Dee Bennett	Stephanie Flowers
Nancy Blout	Vivian Flowers
Irma Brown	Wilhelmina Lewellen
Christene Brownlee	Jacqueline Roberts
Linda Chesterfield	Jamie Scott
Sharon Dobbins	Judy Smith
Joyce Elliott	Wilma Walker
Denise Ennett	Josetta Wilkins

Girl Power: Fun Facts

House of Representatives – Arkansas Origin (Male & Female)

African American Representatives who serve in the Arkansas House (presented in alphabetical order)

Fred Allen - Dist 30

*Denise Ennett -Dist 36

*Vivian Flowers -Dist 17

Kenneth B. Ferguson - Dist 16

David Fielding - Dist 5

Don Glover - Dist 11

Monte Hodges -Dist 55

Fredrick J. Love -Dist 29/Minority Leader

Reginald Murdock -Dist 48

Milton Nicks, Jr -Dist 50

Jay Richardson -Dist 78

*Jamie Scott - Dist 37

*Indicates women who are presently serving

Girl Power: Fun Facts

Music Makes the World Go Round

All forms of music are tools that can unify us. It has a way of starting conversations and can be thought-provoking! Listed below are pioneers in music who are history-makers:

Inez Andrew
Apr 14, 1929 – Dec 19, 2012
A towering gospel singer. She was inducted into the gospel music hall of fame in 2002. She died at age 83 of cancer.

Dr. Maddie Moss Clark
Mar 26, 1925 – Sep 22, 1994
American gospel choir director and mother of *The Clark Singers*. A gospel vocal group headliner, she was the longest surviving international minister of music for the Church of God and Christ.

Natalie Cole
Feb. 6, 1950- Dec 31, 2015
American Singer, Songwriter, Actress, and daughter of Jazz pianist Nat King Cole.

Aretha Franklin
March 25, 1942 – Aug 16, 2018
American Singer, Songwriter, Actress, Pianist, Civil rights Activist and Actress in the movie Blues Brothers.

LaDonna Adrian Gaines (Donna Summers)
Dec 13, 1948 – May 17, 2012
Singer, Song Writer, and Actress – The Queen of Disco!

Aaliyah Dana Haughton
Jan 16, 1979- Aug 25, 2001
Singer, Song Writer, Actress and Model
She gained recognition at the age of ten on Star Search.

Girl Power: Fun Facts

Whitney Houston
Aug. 9, 1963- Feb 11, 2012
Most Awarded Female Act of all time. American Singer recognized by Guinness World Records.

Mahalia Jackson
Oct 26, 1911- Jan 27, 1972
Was an American possessing a contralto voice, she was referred to as The Queen of Gospel- most influential gospel singer in the world. She also was a civil rights activist

Lisa Lopes (Left Eye)
May 27, 1971- April 25, 2002
American Rapper, Singer, Music Producer, and Dancer

Dorothy Norwood
Nov 29, 1935 – Feb 21, 2014
Gospel Singer known as a solo artist until she moved to Chicago then she began singing alongside fellow Gospel Singer Mahalia Jackson

Minnie Rippaton
Nov 8, 1947- Jul 12, 1979
Singer/Songwriter known for her five Octave Coloratura Soprano range. She was known as the Queen of the Whistle register

Nancy Sue Wilson
Feb. 20, 1937- Dec. 13, 2018
American Singer who bridged Jazz and Pop

Deborah and Barak
"The Song of Deborah."
A victory hymn sung about the defeat of Canaanite adversaries by some of the tribes of Israel.
(Judges 5:2-31)

Girl Power: Fun Facts

The Hall of Faith: Heroes and *Sheroes

(The Book of Hebrews chapter 11)

Abel	*Rahab
Enoch	Gideon
Noah	Barak
Abraham	Samson
*Sarah	Jephthah
Isaac	David
Jacob	Samuel
Joseph	Shadrach, Meshach, & Abednego
	(The Book of Daniel chapter 3)
Moses	

*Indicates the only women who are mentioned in the hall of faith in the Bible

Global Empowerment, A Woman's Guide to Liberation

Anjerrio Kameron

In the heart of a woman is the soul of a queen

A visionary agent assigned to a dream

A loyalty committed to achieving success

Unphased by adversity no matter what test

Barriers injustices use to hold back

Collapsed under pressure failed on impact

Nature's imposing unstoppable will

Go where it wants and do what it feels

Extraordinary excellence describes and define

An opulent light with an impeccable shine

Spiritual endowment financed a few

Illustrious careers made dreams come true

Girl Power: Poems

Phyllis Hodges credentials entail

The capacity potential requires to prevail

Business owner carousel-4-life

Loving mother and devoted wife

World-renowned author bestselling book

Made sure living legends were not overlooked

Held seminars to empower and teach

Heart's how to hope and dreams how to reach

Extensive research entitled (8 Years of Unforgettable History)

Was worth all the tears

Michelle Obama, a Nubian queen

First African American and heir to the dream

Became First Lady of The United States

Ignited through a passion inspired by her faith

Princeton's University Collegiate start

Graduated cum lauded Bachelor of Arts

Majored in sociology to help understand

Why peace and prosperity are elusive to man

Minored in the African American plight

Rise from the ashes after burning all night

From Princeton to Harvard's prestigious tree

Graduated Juris Doctor with a law degree

Kamala Harris satisfied her debt

Senator who remember those we forget

Howard University gave her the tools

To litigate laws and legislate rules

Girl Power: Poems

One of ten blacks since the senate begin

To pierce the veil make change from within

Instincts followed its intuition

Strategized planned carried out her mission

Rashida Tlaib and Iilhan Omar

Removed all doubt showed us how far

Democratic emblems jewels to a trust

A value worth more than priceless to us

Exceptional's impressive beacon of light

Envisioned by a brilliance at odds with the night

Indra Nooyi and Melinda Gates

Unequivocally proved impossible was fake

Believers and achievers to whom we respect

Philanthropist to Amazon exec's

Corporate enterprise charitable fund

Equal Opportunity providing income

Ayanna Pressley's enormous contributions

Include civil rights and financial institutions

An activist who believe diversity is key

To issues impelled by political debris

Congressional Representative from Massachusetts State

Confronting white privilege prejudice and hate

Alexandria Cortez congresswoman who ran

On tuition-free colleges and dismantling ICE plans

Graduated Cum Laude Bachelor from B.U

International relations are indebted to you

Advocated platform progressive's gold chair

Job guarantee access to Medicare

Girl Power: Poems

From Serena Williams to Beyonce Knowles

From Simone Biles to her Olympic gold

Not even great can explain these three

So, let us thank God we were blessed to see

From Nancy Pelosi to Oprah Winfrey

Broke through doors that once denied entry

Mona Abaza and Diane Sawyer

Doctors to judges, journalist to lawyers

Iconic pioneers resilience best

Innovative prodigies engineering success

Ambassadors diplomats, architects of grace

Globalizing empowerments ever-changing face

Phenomenals deposits awakening dreams

In the heart of a woman is the soul of a queen

Girl Power: Living Your Dreams

GIRL POWER
Living Your Dreams

Great is the power of all girls
who dare to dream

In a world where their dreams
can become a reality

Rising above the odds to make
their dreams come true

Letting nothing stop their quest
to reach their destiny

Patience is just one of the keys
to being successful in life

Other keys are added as one
overcomes trouble and strife

Women, this power that you have
never, ever let it die

Embrace living your dreams
as long as you have life

Remember, that the struggle for
your success was all worthwhile

Laurence Blinky Walden

Girl Power Affirmations

I AM - Phenomenal	I AM - Wealthy	I AM - Forgiving
I AM - Talented	I AM - Witty	I AM – Valuable
I Am – Resilient	I AM - Beautiful	I AM – Worthy
I Am – Bold	I AM - Healthy	I AM – Spectacular
I AM – Strong	I AM - Fit	I AM – Girl Power
I AM - Smart	I AM – Prospers	I AM – Creative
I AM – Ambitious	I AM – Rich	I AM – Curious
I AM – Wise	I AM – Faithful	I AM - Honest

Girl Power : Write Your Affirmation

I Am _____

I Am _____

I Am _____

I Am _____

I Am _____

I Am _____

I Am _____

I Am _____

I Am _____

I Am _____

I Am _____

Girl Power : Write Your Affirmation

I Am _____

I Am _____

I Am _____

I Am _____

I Am _____

I Am _____

I Am _____

I Am _____

I Am _____

I Am _____

I Am _____

Girl Power: Write Your Affirmation

I Am _____

I Am _____

I Am _____

I Am _____

I Am _____

I Am _____

I Am _____

I Am _____

I Am _____

I Am _____

I Am _____

Girl Power: Affirmations

Girl Power : Write Your Affirmation

I Am _____

I Am _____

I Am _____

I Am _____

I Am _____

I Am _____

I Am _____

I Am _____

I Am _____

I Am _____

I Am _____

Girl Power: Affirmations

El poder de la mujer • • Escribe tu Afirmación

Yo soy _____

Yo soy _____

Yo soy _____

Yo soy _____

Yo soy _____

Yo soy _____

Yo soy _____

Yo soy _____

Yo soy _____

Yo soy _____

Yo soy _____

Girl Power: Affirmations

El poder de la mujer • • Escribe tu Afirmación

Yo soy _____

Yo soy _____

Yo soy _____

Yo soy _____

Yo soy _____

Yo soy _____

Yo soy _____

Yo soy _____

Yo soy _____

Yo soy _____

Yo soy _____

El poder de la mujer • Escribe tu Afirmación

Yo soy _____

Yo soy _____

Yo soy _____

Yo soy _____

Yo soy _____

Yo soy _____

Yo soy _____

Yo soy _____

Yo soy _____

Yo soy _____

Yo soy _____

Girl Power: Affirmations

El poder de la mujer
Escribe tu Afirmación

Yo soy _____

Yo soy _____

Yo soy _____

Yo soy _____

Yo soy _____

Yo soy _____

Yo soy _____

Yo soy _____

Yo soy _____

Yo soy _____

Yo soy _____

The Many Faces of Phyllis

(#DoYouPhylMe)

Available in paperback, hardback and eBook

Order Your Copy Today
Get One for A Friend

Girl Power Products

(Contact the Author to Order)

Figure 1 Flowerpots

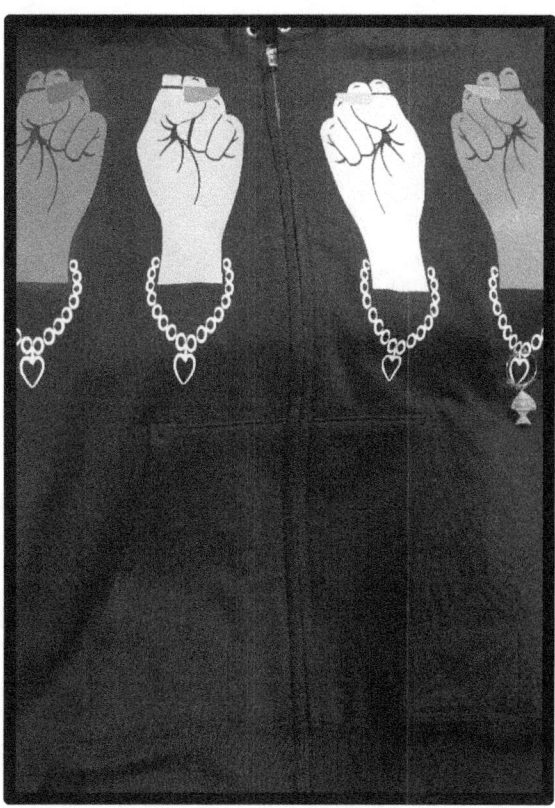

Figure 2 T-shirts and Hoodies

Figure 3 Face Masks

Email: carouselfit4life@gmail.com

Website: doyouphylme.com

Facebook: @GIRL Power

Instagram: @GIRL Power

YouTube: Phyllis Hodges

www.ingramcontent.com/pod-product-compliance
Lightning Source LLC
Chambersburg PA
CBHW082105280426
43661CB00089B/879